MIGUEL BARCLAY'S

ONE POUND MEALS

DELICIOUS FOOD FOR LESS

PHOTOGRAPHY BY DAN JONES

www.onepoundmeals.com

HEADLINE

CONTENTS

As you will see, One Pound Meals is a very relaxed style of cooking, so this book is organised in a similarly laidback manner. There are no chapters or themes. Just flick through the pages and cook whichever dish you fancy and then move on to another, depending on what's in your fridge.

But, as a nod to my Instagram roots and to help you identify types of dish, I have labelled each recipe with hashtags, so if you want to find veggie food, for example, just look out for the veggie hashtags.

To help you find recipes easily, here are all the recipes in this book. Happy cooking!

#VEGETARIAN

#FISHANDSEAFOOD

#CHICKEN

Chicken and Lentil Korma 24

Chicken and
  Mushroom Pie 42

Chicken Caesar Salad 192

Chicken Chow Mein 22

Chicken en Croute 84

Chicken Fajitas 70

Chicken Katsu Curry 56

Chicken Panzanella
  Tray Bake 98

Chicken Stew
  and Dumplings 110

Chicken Tartiflette 40

Chicken Tikka Masala 104

Christmas Dinner 160

Dijon Chicken 114

Faux Confit Chicken 154

'Oven-Fried' Chicken
  and Slaw 58

Roast Chicken Ballotine
  and Potatoes 92

Thai Red Chicken
  Curry 184

Ultimate £1 Roast 144

#MEAT

Balsamic Sausage
  Casserole 46

Cabbage and Bacon
  Conchiglioni 44

Chinese Glazed Pork 112

Club Sandwich 124

Cornish Pasty 198

Ham and Cheese Crêpes 82

Ham and Mushroom Pizza 50

Huevos con Chorizo 100

Keema Bombay
  Potatoes 156

Lahmacun 162

Lamb Kofte with
  Flatbread 178

Lamb Moussaka Stack 94

Lasagne 102

Leek and Bacon Gratin 168

Meatball Marinara 140

Moroccan Lettuce Tacos 180

New York Meatball
  Sandwich 142

Pancake Stack 18

Pork and Spring Onion
  Gyoza 138

Pork Balls and Polenta 68

Pork Chop
  and Colcannon 164

Pork Chop in a Mustard
  and Leek Sauce 200

Pork Loin and Creamy
  Mushroom Pappardelle 88

Pork Schnitzel 34

Pork Stroganoff 118

Pulled Pork Chilli 66

Quiche Lorraine 106

Scotch Eggs 116

Spaghetti Carbonara 186

Stilton-Crusted Pork Loin 76

Toad in the Hole 80

Ultimate £1 Burger 120

INTRODUCING
ONE POUND MEALS

One Pound Meals was born out of my obsession with creating simpler and more straightforward recipes. I had been experimenting with this style of cooking for the past 10 years, it just didn't have a catchy name, until one afternoon I challenged myself to make a paella for £1, posted the dish on Instagram and the rest is history. But, for those of you without Instagram accounts, you may never have seen one of my @onepoundmeals vids before, so let me explain.

Over the years, I must have spent literally hundreds of hours in the kitchen tinkering with recipes. This is my passion. However, I am more of an anti-chef than a chef – instead of adding ingredients to make a dish stand out, I actually take ingredients away and find shortcuts. And this was how One Pound Meals started, from my experimental style of cooking, trying to find the shortest way to tastier food on a budget.

After the success of my paella, I started working to a £1 budget, and found that my unique approach to cooking became a bigger part of the dishes I was creating. As I stripped back dishes even further, recipes became even easier. As I started using only the very best value ingredients, there was so much more crossover between recipes that I found I was wasting less food. My recipes got healthier, too – pre-prepared and processed foods were way too expensive, so everything had to be made from scratch using fresh ingredients. The more the concept developed, the better and better it became.

So, this was how One Pound Meals came about. But, while saving money became a huge part of it, One Pound Meals has evolved into something much bigger than simply cooking on a budget. For me, it's a whole new way of approaching food, a new style of cooking and a new way of life.

I've written this book to show you how you can take the simplest of ingredients and use my straightforward recipes to create mouthwatering dishes on a budget.

Enjoy,

Miguel

WHAT IS A ONE POUND MEAL?

A meal you can totally imagine yourself cooking tonight

There are 5 core principles that make a One Pound Meal, and together they form my overall philosophy and approach to cooking.

1. EASY RECIPES = CONFIDENCE

I always try to take out unnecessary steps and cut corners – that's my style of cooking! I'm not aiming for a Michelin star – my aim is to make a tasty dinner that takes as little time and effort to cook as possible. So I've done the hard work for you, and found the quickest, easiest way to get from a few simple ingredients to the food you see in this book. I want you to feel that you can make these recipes without any hassle, and give you the confidence to try them all.

2. DELICIOUS MEALS = MOTIVATION

I want you to look at these recipe photographs and be inspired to cook them tonight. I hope my recipes look so delicious that when you see what can be achieved for just £1, you'll be motivated to start cooking straight away.

3. EVERYDAY INGREDIENTS = LESS WASTE

There are no fancy or hard-to-find ingredients here. In fact, you probably have a lot of them in your fridge already. One Pound Meals are designed to use a core group of ingredients, and this is the key to eliminating waste. Just start with one recipe, and depending on what you have left over, choose your next recipe accordingly. I want you to bounce around the book on a sort of never-ending random journey as you use up those leftover ingredients. It also means you can plan a week's worth of meals in one go and shop more efficiently.

4. MADE FROM SCRATCH = HEALTHIER

By making food from scratch using fresh produce, you are now in charge of what you eat. When cooking on such a tight budget, pre-prepared and processed foods are just too expensive. No more jars of sauces stuffed with salt, sugar, E-numbers, stabilisers and preservatives – now you can take back control of your diet and know exactly what you are eating.

5. £1 = SAVE MONEY

By shopping clever and cooking creatively, there are huge savings to be made on food. Each recipe has been created using ingredients that add up to £1 or less, but even if you trade up to your favourite cut of meat, or use a slightly more expensive brand, you'll still be quids in. One Pound Meals is a blueprint for how to save money.

ALL RECIPES
ARE FOR A SINGLE
SERVING

More than one person?

Of course you're going to want to impress your friends and family with your
new-found style of cooking, so when feeding more than one person, just
multiply the ingredients. Although each recipe is written for one, they were
designed with friends and family in mind, and my rustic style of cooking is
great if you want to plonk a big pan of food in the middle of the table
for everyone to tuck in.

This is social food that creates a fun atmosphere with plenty
of conversation, so rustle up something fab, invite
your friends round and be proud to be the
centre of attention!

HOW MY
£1 PROMISE WORKS

The only real 'rule' with One Pound Meals is that all the ingredients required to make a dish add up to £1 or less, with the exception of salt, pepper and oil, which almost everyone has to hand.

However, most ingredients are sold in packs that are much larger than you'll need for one portion. So, for the purposes of One Pound Meals, I've only costed the amount I've actually used in the recipe. But, by focusing on important core ingredients, you won't be left with something you'll only use once. Instead, you'll be able to use the remaining ingredients in different recipes, and that way you can navigate your way around the book depending on what you have in your fridge.

CLEVER SHOPPING

To cook meals for £1, you need to shop smart.

The most obvious place to start, and the easiest adjustment to make, is to shop around for the best prices. You don't need to go as overboard as I did, with notebooks and spreadsheets – just being more aware of price differences is a great step in the right direction. I also find myself leaning heavily on budget supermarkets. If you haven't already checked them out, what are you waiting for? Just grab a bag and head down there. The first thing you'll notice is all the fresh veg piled high in boxes. This is exactly what we are after: no expensive packaging, no brand names, just fresh ingredients at rock-bottom prices.

But, if you are particularly loyal to one supermarket or have limited options in your town, you can still plug One Pound Meals into your existing routine; you'll still see significant savings, waste less food and eat delicious meals. Feel free to upgrade your ingredients, too – if you prefer chicken breast to chicken thigh, then do it! I want One Pound Meals to be a flexible approach to food that will slot conveniently into any lifestyle with ease.

Also, one of the big advantages of One Pound Meals is that most ingredients are used in loads of different dishes, so if you want a recipe that uses the rest of that feta cheese, then just go to the index at the back of this book and all the feta recipes are conveniently listed there for you.

COOKING STYLE

I've tried to make my recipes easy, so that you can feel confident cooking my One Pound Meals. This is a relaxed style of cooking, so measurements are purposefully vague. I know that 'a handful' of this or 'a pinch' of that may vary wildly from person to person, but the truth is that it just doesn't matter.

If quantities and methods are mega important, like for dough or pastry, then I'll tell you, but otherwise feel free to chuck in whatever quantities you have left in the fridge. One Pound Meals is an approachable style of cooking that fits around your existing routine, using familiar ingredients that you are probably already comfortable with handling and preparing.

VERSATILE INGREDIENTS

My recipes are based on a core group of common everyday ingredients, which means you'll be able to get the best value from your shopping.

The more common the ingredient the lower the price, so out goes manchego cheese and in comes Cheddar cheese, a worthy substitute that can be used in loads of other recipes. And this point follows nicely on to how waste is cleverly avoided with One Pound Meals. By using the same versatile ingredients across multiple recipes, you're less likely to be stuck with produce that is going out of date and you'll also find that when you open your fridge, you'll have loads of options for dinner.

BASIC UTENSILS

I have been careful to keep things really simple. I don't use fancy kitchen gadgets and have tried to get back to basics using just a knife, a frying pan and a saucepan. Whenever something like breadcrumbs are needed, I don't use a food processor, but improvise by finding clever kitchen hacks like grating stale bread on a cheese grater. It's little things like this that make the One Pound Meals lifestyle achievable for anyone.

A USEFUL STORE CUPBOARD

Don't worry, I'm not going to ask you to buy a huge list of 'essentials'. With One Pound Meals you'll just accumulate them slowly as you start cooking the recipes. As with the fresh produce, I've focused on common ingredients that can be used in multiple dishes. Paprika is a perfect example of a common spice that is extremely versatile and I've used it in loads of recipes, from my Thai Red Curry to my Pork Stroganoff and Moroccan Spiced Veg. This is a great way to reduce the number of random jars of spices you buy that just sit in your cupboard untouched.

Along with spices, you'll also be investing in basic essentials like stock cubes and tins of tomatoes. These are super-cheap, last for ages and enable you to cook great dishes from scratch. So just relax and watch your cupboard slowly grow into a huge asset that will help you create delicious meals on a budget.

MY FAVOURITE ONE POUND MEALS INGREDIENTS

MEAT & FISH

MINCED LAMB – soooo tasty, maybe the tastiest meat of all?

MINCED BEEF – versatile and robust in flavour

MINCED PORK – a more delicate and subtle meat

CHICKEN THIGHS – these taste better than chicken breasts

CHICKEN LEGS – versatile and great for stuffing

CHICKEN DRUMSTICKS – cooking meat on the bone makes it so much juicier

BACON – make sure it's smoked and streaky

PORK CHOPS – the most luxurious yet economical cut of meat

PORK BELLY – needs some care and attention, but the result is well worth it

SAUSAGES – a nice treat once in a while

CHORIZO – make use of the paprika-infused oils that come out when you pan-fry it

PRAWNS – a great, affordable seafood treat

TINNED CRAB – tastes super-fresh. Get whole chunks, not shredded crab

TINNED SARDINES – you'll always have a back-up plan with these in your cupboard

VEGETABLES

POTATOES – my favourite carb: filling and delicious

AUBERGINE – great value and very versatile

SPINACH – don't overcook it, just let it wilt

PEPPER – best when slightly caramelised for that extra depth of flavour

ROCKET – my favourite salad leaf, lovely and peppery

MUSHROOMS – I love them just as much as meat, and I LOVE meat

ONIONS – you can't cook without onions, they are the base of most dishes

TOMATOES – loaded with vitamin C

BUTTERNUT SQUASH – amazing value, just compare its size against a similarly-priced avocado

SPRING ONIONS – great as a garnish, with a subtler flavour than standard onions

GREEN BEANS – they're best when they still have some bite, so don't overcook them

CARROTS – another essential veg that helps form a base to many dishes

CABBAGE – do not boil it! Just pan-fry it in a splash of oil with salt and pepper

LETTUCE – the most popular salad leaf ever!

ASPARAGUS – the price of this delicacy plummets when the season is in full swing

KALE – pairs well with lots of pepper

GARLIC – essential for most styles of cooking

STORE CUPBOARD

SALT & PEPPER – needs no explanation

OLIVE OIL – the perfect all-round oil

VEGETABLE OIL – cheaper alternative to olive oil

TINNED CHOPPED TOMATOES – I don't think I could survive without these

PASSATA – just liquidised chopped tomatoes

DIJON MUSTARD – has an amazing complex flavour that can transform a dish

PLAIN FLOUR – use to make wraps and thicken homemade sauces

SELF-RAISING FLOUR – a nice little hack to make pancakes and dumplings

'00' FLOUR – used for pizza dough and pasta. This is a game changer. Invest and reap the rewards

STOCK CUBES – an essential part of One Pound Meals when building depth of flavour with just a few ingredients

GRAVY GRANULES – a nice little cheat. Don't feel guilty, I use them all the time!

POLENTA – doesn't get the credit it deserves. Give it a try, you'll love it

DRIED PASTA – there are so many different varieties. A great blank canvas to create the flavours you want

RISOTTO RICE – good for bulking out small amounts of leftover food

BASMATI RICE – give your dishes a bit of excitement by switching up your usual rice to basmati

LONG-GRAIN RICE – turn it into something spectacular like my shrimp fried rice

SESAME OIL – a secret ingredient that will transform your cooking

SOY SAUCE – essential for Chinese cooking

BALSAMIC VINEGAR – has a very strong flavour that helps cut through the richness of a dish

PUFF PASTRY – switch things up and make a pie (keep pastry in the fridge)

STUFFING MIX – another great shortcut

DRIED OREGANO – an essential herb for Italian cooking

PAPRIKA – very versatile and has a little bit of kick to it

CURRY POWDER – the one Indian spice you definitely need

GROUND CUMIN – I use this for my Moroccan inspired dishes

CAJUN SPICE MIX – a great cheat to get a blend of Southern fried spices

DRIED LENTILS – cook them gently to release their creaminess

TINNED KIDNEY BEANS – good for bulking out a chilli

TINNED CHICKPEAS – a great alternative to traditional carbs

DAIRY & EGGS

PARMESAN – has a salty depth of flavour that is needed for pasta and gnocchi

MOZZARELLA – creamy and soft, it melts perfectly on pizzas

CHEDDAR – the king of cheese. Always try to get mature Cheddar

STILTON – packed with a powerful flavour (a little goes a long way)

FETA – salty and perfect to crumble on top of dishes

SINGLE CREAM – essential for making creamy sauces

CRÈME FRAÎCHE – my guilty pleasure. I dollop it on anything

MAYO – who can be bothered to make it from scratch?

EGGS – used in loads of my One Pound Meals

JOIN THE
ONE POUND MEALS
REVOLUTION

So what are you waiting for? All you need to do is turn to any page in this book and you can start your One Pound Meals journey today. This could be a turning point in your cooking! Just use this book as your guide to change the way you cook and think about food, and save yourself a small fortune in the process.

PANCAKE STACK

A tall stack of pancakes always looks impressive, so by using this thicker American-style batter recipe, you will be able to recreate exactly the same effect at home. This New York-style brunch manages to bring together both sweet and savoury to create a delicious weekend treat.

To make 1 portion

75g self-raising flour

15g caster sugar

1 large egg, lightly beaten

60ml milk

10g butter

3 rashers of smoked streaky bacon

Runny honey, for drizzling

To cook

In a jug, whisk together the flour, sugar, egg and milk. Melt the butter (this takes just 10 seconds in the microwave) and pour it into the mixture.

Fry the bacon in a pan until crispy. In a separate pre-heated pan, start to cook the pancakes by pouring a small amount of batter into the centre. After about 15 seconds, flip the pancake using a spatula and cook it evenly on both sides. Transfer to a plate and repeat with the rest of the batter.

Stack up the pancakes as high as you can, top with the crispy bacon and drizzle over some honey.

SHAKSHUKA

This dish has fantastic Middle Eastern flavours that really complement the vibrant and fresh ingredients. It is such a simple dish to make and great to eat as a healthy brunch with a chunk of crusty bread to mop up the sauce.

To make 1 portion

1 tsp cumin seeds

½ red onion, sliced

¼ yellow pepper, sliced

200g chopped tomatoes (from a 400g tin)

1 egg

Chunk of crusty bread

Olive oil

Salt and pepper

To cook

Toast the cumin seeds in a small dry pan, over a medium heat, until they start to pop, then add a splash of olive oil and the sliced onion. Once the onion starts to soften, add the sliced pepper and chopped tomatoes. Season generously and simmer until the sauce thickens.

Make a small crater in the tomato mixture using the back of a spoon and crack the egg into it, place a lid on the pan and continue to simmer gently until the white is cooked but the yolk is still runny.

Serve in the pan and don't forget to mop up all the juices with some bread.

CHICKEN CHOW MEIN

This authentic-tasting chow mein dish will definitely compete with your local takeaway. It was hugely popular on Instagram and immediately became a One Pound Meals favourite. If you have leftover meat or veg, you can also use this recipe as a template to create different versions of chow mein, but whatever you do, remember the sesame oil: this stuff will elevate your Chinese cooking to the next level.

To make 1 portion

1 chicken thigh, de-boned

1 sheet of dried noodles

Pinch of dried chilli flakes

1 garlic clove, sliced

¼ red onion, sliced

¼ green pepper, diced

1 egg

Sesame oil

Soy sauce

Vegetable oil

Salt and pepper

To cook

Season and gently pan-fry the chicken thigh skin-side down in a splash of vegetable oil over a medium heat for 7 minutes, then a further 7 minutes on the other side, until golden brown and cooked through.

While the chicken is frying, cook the noodles in salted boiling water according to the packet instructions.

Remove the chicken from the pan, turn the heat up to high and add more oil if needed. Throw in the chilli flakes, garlic and red onion. Season, then stir-fry for a minute, before adding the diced pepper. After another minute, drain the noodles and add them to the pan, then slice the chicken before adding that too. Scoop everything to one side of the pan and crack the egg into the empty side. Start to fry the egg and, once it is half cooked,

scramble it with a wooden spoon and mix it with the noodles. Add a splash of sesame oil and a splash of soy sauce and serve in a bowl.

CHICKEN & LENTIL KORMA

This certainly is not chicken korma as you'd know it, but through my use of korma spices and the creaminess of the lentils, it is probably the best way to describe this slightly unusual dish. Crisping up the chicken with a pan-fried korma marinade creates a great contrast in texture to the soft and creamy korma-spiced lentils.

To make 1 portion

1 chicken thigh, de-boned

3 tsp korma curry powder

¼ onion, sliced

1 garlic clove, sliced

2 handfuls of red lentils

200ml water

Handful of spinach

Olive oil

Salt and pepper

To cook

Season the chicken thigh and coat it in 1 teaspoon of the korma curry powder and a splash of oil, then pan-fry it skin-side down over a medium heat for 7 minutes, then a further 7 minutes on the other side, until cooked through.

Meanwhile, fry the onion in a saucepan in a splash of oil and, once softened, add the garlic and continue to fry for a minute. Add the lentils, water and the remaining korma curry powder. Simmer, uncovered, over a medium heat for about 15 minutes, or until the sauce is nice and thick but the lentils still retain a bit of bite. Remove from the heat, taste and season if needed, and stir in the spinach.

Cut the chicken into cubes and stir it into the lentils to create your chicken and lentil korma.

CRAB LINGUINI

Crab linguini is a classic seaside holiday dish that is surprisingly easy to replicate at home. With tinned crab available in most supermarkets at such a low price, there are no more excuses – you could be eating this in exactly the time it takes to boil a kettle, plus 8 minutes to cook the pasta.

To make 1 portion

25g dried linguini

Handful of cherry tomatoes, quartered

1 garlic clove, sliced

1 tsp dried chilli flakes

1 tbsp tinned crab

Lemon wedge

Pinch of dried (or chopped fresh) parsley

Olive oil

Salt and pepper

To cook

Bring a pan of salted water to the boil and cook the linguini until al dente.

Meanwhile, gently pan-fry the cherry tomatoes in a generous glug of olive oil over a medium heat. After 3 minutes, add the garlic, the chilli flakes and then the crab. Continue to fry for a couple of minutes until the garlic just starts to brown, then remove from the heat and squeeze some lemon juice into the pan and add the parsley. Season with salt and pepper, then add the linguini straight from the boiling water into the pan using tongs, along with a few splashes of the pasta cooking water.

Give it a little stir and serve straight away!

INSIDE-OUT VEGETABLE MOUSSAKA

I just love this dish – it's so cool! And its fun presentation makes it look really exciting, so next time you have to impress a vegetarian, why not serve them this unforgettable inside-out moussaka.

To make 1 portion

1 aubergine

½ onion, roughly diced

1 garlic clove, sliced

1 tsp dried oregano, plus extra to garnish

1 tsp ground cumin

200g chopped tomatoes (from a 400g tin)

½ tsp butter

½ tsp plain flour

30ml milk

Small handful of grated Cheddar cheese

1 egg, beaten

Olive oil

Salt and pepper

To cook

Preheat your oven to 190°C/gas mark 5.

Slice the side off the aubergine lengthways and scoop out the middle using a knife to cut sections away from the inside and a spoon to scoop them out. Leave the sides about 1cm thick, so that they can hold the filling.

Fry the onion in a pan over a medium heat in a splash of olive oil until soft, then dice the scooped out bits of aubergine and add them to the pan with a little more olive oil. Season well and continue frying until the onion starts to brown, then add the garlic, oregano and cumin and fry until the garlic starts to brown.

Add the chopped tomatoes and simmer for 10 minutes until the sauce is thickened, then fill the aubergine with this mixture.

Meanwhile, to make the cheesy topping, melt the butter in a saucepan over a medium heat, then mix in the flour to form a paste. Slowly whisk in the milk and cook for 1 minute until a sauce has formed, then remove from the heat and stir in the grated cheese. Mix in half the beaten egg (keep the rest of the beaten egg in the fridge for another recipe) then spread the mixture on top of the stuffed aubergine.

Cook on a baking tray in the oven for 30 minutes, or until the top is golden brown, then scatter with extra oregano to serve.

SHRIMP FRIED RICE

The secret to this dish is the sesame oil, which replicates the authentic Chinese flavour that home-cooked dishes often lack. So, why not buy yourself a bottle, transform your cooking, stop ordering takeaways and save yourself a fortune!

To make 1 portion

1 mug of water

½ mug of long-grain rice

Sesame oil

Handful of cooked and peeled prawns

1 egg

2 spring onions, chopped

Soy sauce

To cook

In a saucepan, bring the water and rice to the boil, cover and simmer gently. When the rice is cooked and has absorbed all the water, tip it into a bowl and allow to cool to room temperature (or refrigerate).

When the rice is cold, heat a wok (or large saucepan) over a high heat and add a splash of sesame oil along with the rice. As the rice starts to fry – keep stirring so that it doesn't burn at the bottom – add the prawns.

Scoop everything to one side of the pan and crack the egg into the empty side. Start to fry the egg and, once it is half cooked, scramble it with a wooden spoon and mix it in with the rice. Add the chopped spring onions and a final splash of sesame oil, then mix it all together over the heat and serve in a bowl with a splash of soy sauce.

BUTTERNUT SQUASH RISOTTO

The butternut squash in this dish gives it a lovely subtly sweet taste and luxurious gooey texture. And, if you are wondering what to do with all those pumpkins at Halloween, why not substitute the butternut squash in this recipe for pumpkin? Whatever you do, make sure you keep some of that amazing paprika-infused oil from the oven tray to drizzle over the risotto at the end. If you love this, try my Spiced Butternut Squash Soup (see page 172).

To make 1 portion

¼ butternut squash, peeled and roughly diced

1 tbsp paprika

¼ onion, diced

Handful of Arborio risotto rice (approx. 125g)

500ml boiling water

1 vegetable stock cube

Knob of butter

Small handful of grated parmesan (approx. 10g)

Olive oil

Salt and pepper

To cook

Preheat your oven to 190°C/gas mark 5.

Toss the squash in a roasting tray or ovenproof dish with a generous glug of olive oil and the paprika, and season with salt and pepper. Add a few of the butternut squash seeds too – they become deliciously crunchy in the oven. Roast for 40 minutes until slightly caramelised, with a soft and gooey texture.

When the butternut squash is cooked, stick the kettle on and get started on the risotto.

Pan-fry the diced onion gently in a splash of olive oil. Add a few chunks of the roasted butternut squash and, as the risotto cooks, it will gently break down into a pulp. Before the onion starts to brown, add the rice and season with a pinch of salt and pepper.

Add 100ml of the hot water from the pre-boiled kettle and crumble in the stock cube. Stir the rice over a medium heat as the stock cube dissolves.

After a couple of minutes, the rice will have absorbed most of the water. At this point add another 100ml of hot water from the kettle and continue stirring. Keep adding hot water in small amounts as you continue to stir, until the risotto rice is tender but firm to the bite.

Remove from the heat, add the butter and grated parmesan and stir. When the butter and parmesan have disappeared, add the remaining chunks of roasted squash, scatter over a few of the toasted seeds and then drizzle over some of the paprika-infused oil from the roasting tray.

PORK SCHNITZEL

The art of One Pound Meals is to keep food interesting and varied throughout the week. So, when you need to find a different way to prepare a pork loin, look no further than Germany and its world-famous schnitzel.

To make 1 portion

A few new potatoes

1 pork loin chop

1 tbsp plain flour

1 egg, beaten

Handful of breadcrumbs (grated stale bread)

A few slices of red onion

Lemon wedge

Olive oil

Salt and pepper

To cook

Boil the new potatoes in a pan of salted water until cooked all the way through.

Place the pork chop between two sheets of greaseproof paper and bash it with a rolling pin to flatten it out to a thickness of about 5mm.

Place the flour and some seasoning in one bowl, the beaten egg in another bowl, and the breadcrumbs and some seasoning in a third bowl.

Season the pork then dust it with the flour, dip it in the beaten egg and cover in the seasoned breadcrumbs.

Pan-fry the schnitzel over a low heat in a splash of olive oil, until the breadcrumbs are golden and the pork is cooked all the way through.

When the potatoes are cooked and are still hot, slice them and mix them with the red onion, adding a squeeze of lemon juice, and serve alongside the schnitzel.

CAULIFLOWER KEDGEREE

Kedgeree is an old-school classic, but I've brought it into the 21st century with a One Pound Meals twist! By using tiny grains of cauliflower instead of rice, and chunky cauliflower florets pan-fried in Indian spices instead of haddock, this dish has been transformed into a modern vegetarian recipe.

To make 1 portion

1 egg

¼ cauliflower

2 tsp korma curry powder

1 spring onion, chopped

50ml milk

Olive oil

Salt and pepper

To cook

Bring a saucepan of water to the boil and cook the egg for 10 minutes.

Chop about 8 small florets from the cauliflower and pan-fry them in a splash of oil over a medium heat with 1 teaspoon of the korma curry powder and a pinch of salt.

Meanwhile, finely chop the remaining cauliflower into tiny pieces about the size of rice grains (you can do this by hand or in a food processor).

Once the florets have started to brown, add the spring onion and continue to fry for a couple of minutes. Next, add the finely chopped cauliflower, milk and remaining korma curry powder. Season and simmer gently over a medium heat for about 10 minutes, until the milk has disappeared, then remove from the heat, peel the boiled egg, quarter it and add it to your finished dish.

CRAB MAC & CHEESE

Crab? In a One Pound Meal? It's a little-known secret that you can get the most amazing tinned crab in supermarkets. Make sure you get the whole chunks and not the shredded stuff, and give this dish a try. I have used it to create a decadent twist on an already rich and luxurious mature Cheddar mac and cheese.

To make I portion

100g macaroni

½ onion, finely diced

1 garlic clove, sliced

Pinch of dried chilli flakes

Squirt of English mustard

1 tsp butter

1 tsp plain flour

100ml milk

Handful of grated mature Cheddar cheese

1 tbsp tinned crab

Olive oil

Salt and pepper

To cook

Preheat your oven to 190°C/gas mark 5.

Bring a pan of salted water to the boil and cook the macaroni until al dente.

Meanwhile, gently fry the onion with a splash of oil in a saucepan over a medium heat. After a few minutes, when the onion starts to turn translucent, add the garlic and continue to fry until the garlic starts to brown. Add the dried chilli flakes and mustard, stir, then add the butter. As soon as the butter melts, add the flour and stir until the flour has disappeared. At this point add the milk very slowly, while continuing to stir.

Once you have a thick sauce, remove from the heat and stir in the grated cheese. Taste and season if required.

Next, add the crab and drained macaroni to the sauce, stir, and transfer to an ovenproof dish. Cook for 30 minutes, until golden brown, and enjoy on a cold winter's day!

CHICKEN TARTIFLETTE

I've slightly tweaked this traditional French recipe to make it a more substantial meal. Instead of subtle and delicate layering, I've created one bold filling with chicken and bacon, then topped it with a chunky potato lid that crisps up beautifully in the oven. In fact, it now hardly bears any resemblance to the original dish, oops!

To make 1 portion

3 new potatoes, cut into 3mm-thick slices

1 chicken thigh, skin removed, de-boned, and diced

¼ onion, sliced

2 rashers of smoked streaky bacon, diced

1 garlic clove, sliced

1 tsp plain flour

50ml milk

Small handful of grated Cheddar cheese

Handful of spinach

Olive oil

Salt and pepper

To cook

Preheat your oven to 190°C/gas mark 5.

Cook the sliced potatoes in a pan of boiling water for 10 minutes to soften.

Season the diced chicken well, then fry in a splash of olive oil in a saucepan (or ovenproof dish) over a medium heat for about 5 minutes. When the chicken starts to brown, add the onion and bacon. When the bacon starts to crisp up, add the garlic and continue to fry for a minute. Next, add the flour and stir it in for a minute. Then, add the milk, little by little, stirring continuously, to create a sauce.

When all the milk is added, throw in most of the grated cheese and stir it into the sauce. Remove from the heat, stir in the spinach and transfer the mixture to an ovenproof dish (if you were using a saucepan).

Arrange the potato slices over the top and sprinkle with the remaining cheese.

Cook in the oven for 25 minutes, or until the potatoes are a nice golden brown.

CHICKEN & MUSHROOM PIE

By using pre-made puff pastry, all the hard work has been done for you. I'm not sure pies get much easier than this, so it is definitely worth having a go. An all-time classic British pie for under £1, and with almost no effort? What have you got to lose?

To make 1 portion

1 chicken thigh, de-boned, skin removed and diced

¼ onion, sliced

A few mushrooms, sliced

2 tsp plain flour

125ml milk

Sheet of puff pastry

Olive oil

Salt and pepper

To cook

Preheat your oven to 190°C/gas mark 5.

Season the chicken, then pan-fry it in a splash of olive oil over a medium heat for about 5 minutes. When the chicken starts to brown, add the onion and mushrooms. Continue to fry until the mushrooms start to brown, then stir in the flour. Slowly add the milk, while stirring continuously, to create a creamy sauce. Taste and season once more, then transfer to a small ovenproof dish.

Cut a piece of puff pastry to fit the dish and cover the chicken and mushroom filling, then cook the pie in the oven for about 25 minutes, or until the pastry is a lovely golden brown colour. Remove from the oven and dig in!

CABBAGE & BACON CONCHIGLIONI

Here's a simple dish that hits some great flavour notes and can be knocked up in under 10 minutes. Try to get a little bit of colour on the cabbage and you'll notice the extra depth of flavour, then add plenty of olive oil to bring the dish together – it will create a dressing of sorts, as it gets infused by the pan-fried garlic.

To make 1 portion

Handful of dried conchiglioni pasta

3 rashers of smoked streaky bacon, roughly diced

1 garlic clove, sliced

A few Savoy cabbage leaves, shredded

Olive oil

Salt and pepper

To cook

Bring a pan of salted water to the boil and cook the pasta until al dente.

Meanwhile, gently pan-fry the bacon in a splash of olive oil over a medium heat. When the bacon starts to colour, throw in the garlic and cabbage. Season well with plenty of salt and pepper, then add more olive oil and continue to fry until the garlic starts to brown.

Remove the pan from the heat, drain the cooked pasta and add it to the pan, then mix everything together to create your cabbage and bacon conchiglioni.

BALSAMIC SAUSAGE CASSEROLE

Sometimes stews and casseroles can be a bit too predictable. So, why not change it up for once? This exciting, zingy modern twist on a classic casserole has interesting and uplifting flavours. By using sausages instead of the usual cuts of meat, you now have pockets of deeper and more interesting flavours that can handle a generous glug of balsamic vinegar. Give it a try and you'll see exactly what I'm talking about.

To make 1 portion

2 sausages

½ red onion, sliced

½ yellow pepper, sliced

1 tsp plain flour

200g chopped tomatoes (from a 400g tin)

1 beef stock cube

1 tbsp balsamic vinegar

Olive oil

Salt and pepper

To cook

Grab a casserole dish or a saucepan, and fry the sausages in a splash of oil over a medium heat until cooked through and nicely browned on the outside.

Remove the sausages from the pan, cut them into chunks, then return them to the pan along with the onion, yellow pepper and a splash of olive oil. Season well and fry for a few minutes until the onions are soft and starting to colour. Add the flour and stir for 30 seconds, then add the chopped tomatoes, crumble in the stock cube, add the balsamic vinegar and just enough water to cover the ingredients. Simmer for about 15 minutes, stirring occasionally, until the sauce is nice and thick, then remove from the heat and serve.

HAM & MUSHROOM PIZZA

Pizzas are so much fun to make at home, and they are totally worth the effort. These are Italian-style pizzas, exactly the same type you see in posh restaurants with wood-fired ovens. So, learn to make this simple recipe and you'll have £1 pizzas whenever you want and save yourself a small fortune on takeaways! You need to leave the dough to rise overnight so plan ahead.

To make 1 portion

½ tsp dried yeast (approx.1g)

100ml water

180g Italian '00' pasta flour, plus extra for dusting

5g salt

3 tbsp passata

½ mozzarella ball, sliced

1 slice of ham, roughly torn

A few slices of mushroom

Salt and pepper

To cook

Firstly, in a jug or bowl, dissolve the dried yeast in the water.

Then, in a bowl, using a tablespoon, mix the flour, water and salt to create a dough. Tip it onto your worktop and knead for 10 minutes until you have a smooth, elastic dough.

Place the dough in a bowl, cover with cling film and leave overnight to rise at room temperature.

The next day, using a tablespoon, scoop the sides of the sticky dough away from the bowl and tip the dough ball onto a floured worktop. Using your fingertips and plenty of flour for dusting, press down into the dough, gently shaping it into a circle, or just use a rolling pin if you find it easier. Grab your biggest frying pan, and when the dough is roughly the same width as your frying pan, place it in the pan and use your fingers to stretch it into a circle that covers the whole base.

Place the pan on your hob over maximum heat, spread the passata over the base while it is cooking and turn on your grill.

After a minute or so, lift up the edge of the pizza, and once the base is starting to colour, add the mozzarella, ham and mushroom slices. Season, then immediately transfer to the grill and cook the top of the pizza.

Once the pizza is browned at the edges and the cheese is bubbling, add some ground black pepper to finish.

FIORENTINA PIZZA

Looking for a more adventurous pizza? Then try this vegetarian fiorentina pizza with an egg in the middle. Again, note that the dough needs to rise overnight.

To make 1 portion

1 quantity of dough (see opposite)

3 tbsp passata

½ mozzarella ball, sliced

Small handful of spinach

1 egg

Small handful of parmesan shavings

Olive oil

Salt and pepper

To cook

Make the dough following the instructions in the recipe opposite, up to the point where you spread it with the passata while it's cooking.

Once the base is starting to colour, add the mozzarella and spinach and crack the egg into the centre. Season, add a small splash of olive oil, then immediately transfer to the grill and cook the top of the pizza.

Once the pizza is cooked, sprinkle over the parmesan shavings and some ground black pepper to finish.

AUBERGINE PARMIGIANA

Parmigiana is an Italian classic! But here I have used my own interpretation of the dish to create a more substantial and elaborate main meal. Traditionally served as a starter with floppy slices of aubergine hidden under tomato sauce, I have turned the whole dish on its head and created a platform for the aubergine to take centre stage.

To make 1 portion

½ red onion, diced

1 garlic clove, sliced

200g chopped tomatoes (from a 400g tin)

1 tsp dried oregano

½ aubergine (from 1 aubergine halved lengthways)

½ mozzarella ball, sliced

Olive oil

Salt and pepper

To cook

Preheat your oven to 190°C/gas mark 5.

To create the sauce, gently pan-fry the onion for a few minutes in a splash of olive oil over a medium heat, then add the garlic. After a few minutes, when the garlic is starting to brown, add the chopped tomatoes, season with salt and pepper and add half the oregano. Simmer for 2 minutes, then tip the sauce into an ovenproof dish.

Place the aubergine half cut-side down on a board. Use a sharp knife to cut deep V-shaped slits across it every 2.5cm or so. Be careful that you only cut 90 per cent of the way through the aubergine so that you still have one whole piece. Dust each slice of mozzarella with oregano and season with salt and pepper. Squeeze a slice into each slit.

Place the aubergine in the middle of the sauce and oven-roast for 30 minutes, or until the aubergine is fully cooked and the cheese is melted and starting to colour nicely.

Remove from the oven and serve with a little splash of oil over the top.

CHICKEN KATSU CURRY

This was the dish that kick-started my @onepoundmeals Instagram account. It went viral, and one week later I was cooking it live on *This Morning* with Ruth and Eamonn! It seems that everybody knows somebody whose favourite dish is katsu curry, so learning to make this dish is an important life skill. But, for this dish to work, I had to really simplify the sauce, and luckily, using a French technique of thickening sauces with flour, I made the breakthrough that turned this seemingly impossible dish into a One Pound Meal. People liked it and the rest is history!

To make 1 portion

1 tbsp plain flour, plus 1 tsp

1 egg, beaten

Handful of breadcrumbs (grated stale bread)

1 chicken thigh, skin removed and de-boned

½ mug of basmati rice

1 mug of water

1 tsp curry powder

75ml water

Squirt of honey

Splash of soy sauce

1 spring onion, sliced

Olive oil

Salt and pepper

To cook

Place the flour and some seasoning in one bowl, the beaten egg in another bowl, and the breadcrumbs and some seasoning in a third bowl. Dust the chicken thigh in the flour, dip it in the egg, then coat it in the breadcrumbs.

Gently pan-fry the chicken in a splash of olive oil over a low heat. Turn it over once when the underside becomes a lovely golden brown and cook the other side, making sure that the chicken is cooked through at the end.

Meanwhile, put the rice and water in a saucepan, bring to the boil and simmer gently, with the lid on, for about 7 minutes. When all the water has been absorbed, the rice is ready to serve.

As the chicken and rice cook, make the sauce by mixing the curry powder with the teaspoon of flour and a splash of oil in a pan over a medium heat. Keep stirring and gradually add the water, then as the sauce comes together, add the honey and soy sauce. The final sauce should have a very thick gravy consistency and be dark brown.

Serve by slicing the chicken and placing it on a bed of fluffy rice, scatter over the sliced spring onion, then drizzle the sauce over the top.

'OVEN-FRIED' CHICKEN & SLAW

By using the secret ingredient of a beaten egg in the coating, this recipe is able to recreate the delicious taste and texture of your favourite fried chicken but using an oven. This also makes my 'oven-fried' chicken a much healthier alternative. For the southern fried seasoning, I have a great One Pound Meals money-saving (and space-saving) cheat for you! We all know that the Colonel has a secret blend of 11 herbs and spices… well, a jar of Cajun spice is a good substitute!

To make 1 portion

3 tbsp plain flour

1 tbsp Cajun spice blend

1 egg

4 chicken drumsticks

Small wedge of white cabbage, finely shredded

½ carrot, finely shredded

¼ red onion, thinly sliced

Squirt of mayonnaise

Olive oil

Salt and pepper

To cook

Preheat your oven to 190°C/gas mark 5.

In one bowl, combine the flour, Cajun spice and some salt and pepper. In another bowl, beat the egg. Evenly coat the chicken drumsticks in the seasoned flour, then coat them in the egg, and then the seasoned flour once again.

Arrange them in a greased ovenproof dish and cook in the oven for about 30 minutes, until golden brown and cooked all the way through. For an extra crispy coating, drizzle with a little olive oil about halfway through cooking.

Meanwhile, to make the coleslaw, combine the cabbage, carrot and red onion in a bowl and mix with the mayo, some cracked black pepper and a little salt. Watch out that you don't over-salt the slaw – you only need the tiniest amount.

When the chicken is cooked, serve with the slaw and enjoy!

BUTTERNUT SQUASH TAGLIATELLE

Butternut squash turns so thick and creamy when oven baked that you can get away with using it as the only additional ingredient in a pasta dish. It has a gorgeous sweet but savoury flavour and is the perfect ingredient to create a luxuriously rich meal.

To make 1 portion

¼ butternut squash, peeled and roughly diced

Handful of dried tagliatelle pasta

Olive oil

Salt and pepper

To cook

Preheat your oven to 190°C/gas mark 5.

Bake the butternut squash in an ovenproof dish with plenty of olive oil, salt and pepper for about 40 minutes until soft and gooey.

When the butternut squash is cooked, cook the pasta in a saucepan of salted boiling water until al dente.

While the pasta cooks, transfer the baked butternut squash to a frying pan over a medium heat, then mash it with the back of a fork and add a glug of olive oil, salt and plenty of pepper. Drain the cooked pasta and add it to the pan, mixing everything together to form a rich and luxurious coated pasta.

SARDINES & SALSA VERDE

When you start getting the winter blues, this dish will take you right back to happy holiday thoughts. So, next time you see sardines at the supermarket, stock up! They last for ages and are a great standby ingredient. They are also packed full of omega-3 fats and taste amazing.

To make 1 portion

1 potato, peeled and chopped

1 tbsp plain flour

120g tin of whole sardines in oil, drained

1 tsp Dijon mustard

1 tsp dried (or fresh chopped) parsley

Olive oil

Salt and pepper

To cook

Cook the chopped potato in salted boiling water until soft, then drain and mash with a splash of olive oil and a pinch of salt.

Season the flour with salt and pepper, and lightly dust the tinned sardines in the flour. Heat a pan over a medium heat and fry them gently with a generous glug of olive oil for 5 minutes, until the skin turns a lovely crispy golden brown.

Meanwhile, to make the salsa verde, combine the Dijon mustard, parsley and 4 teaspoons of olive oil in a small bowl and season with salt and pepper.

Serve the sardines on a bed of the mashed potato with the salsa verde on the side.

STILTON PORTABELLA

Mushrooms are wonderful stuffed, and their rich earthy flavours especially complement my stilton and spring onion stuffing. I like to sprinkle extra breadcrumbs on top for a little crunch, to create a nice variation in texture.

To make 1 portion

2 large cap mushrooms

25g stilton cheese, crumbled

Small handful of breadcrumbs
  (grated stale bread)

1 spring onion, finely chopped

Handful of rocket

Olive oil

Salt and pepper

To cook

Preheat your oven to 190°C/gas mark 5.

Lightly brush the mushrooms with olive oil and bake in the oven on a baking tray for 10 minutes, until dark in colour and cooked.

Meanwhile, make the stuffing. Using your fingers, squash together the crumbled stilton, half the breadcrumbs and the chopped spring onion to create a doughy consistency. Remove the mushrooms from the oven and fill each mushroom with the stuffing.

Add a splash of olive oil and some salt and pepper to the remaining breadcrumbs and sprinkle them over the filled mushrooms.

Cook under a hot grill until the breadcrumbs are golden and the cheese is bubbling, then serve on a bed of rocket.

PULLED PORK CHILLI

If you substitute minced beef for homemade pulled pork, you'll get the best chilli ever. And by slow-cooking the chilli, the flavour gets to develop for much longer; you'll certainly notice the difference. Don't be tempted to leave out the crème fraîche – it plays an important part in balancing the flavours as it gives a fresh zing to a very earthy and hearty dish.

To make 1 portion

2 pork belly slices (approx. 150g total weight)

1 red onion, thickly sliced

1 garlic clove, sliced

1 tsp ground cumin

1 tsp paprika

1 tsp plain flour

200g chopped tomatoes (from a 400g tin)

1 beef stock cube

150ml water

200g kidney beans (from a 400g tin, drained)

1 tbsp crème fraîche

A few thin slices of spring onion tips

Olive oil

Salt and pepper

To cook

Start by seasoning and frying the pork belly slices in a saucepan with a splash of oil. When they are nicely browned, add the onion and then a few minutes later the garlic. As the garlic just starts to brown, add the cumin, paprika and flour. Stir until all the flour disappears, then add the chopped tomatoes, crumble in the stock cube and add the water.

Simmer gently over a low heat for 1½ hours with the lid on then, 10 minutes before serving, add the kidney beans and simmer with the lid off. If you find there's not enough liquid in the pan, add a splash more water.

Using two forks, tear the pork apart into chunks, then serve the chilli with a big dollop of crème fraîche and sliced spring onion tips.

PORK BALLS & POLENTA

Polenta is a very under-appreciated ingredient in the UK, but with such an amazing flavour and such an economical price, I knew I had to include it in my book. In this recipe I flavour the polenta with mature Cheddar cheese and when it is coupled with these amazing pork meatballs, this dish shows us that exciting and interesting food doesn't have to cost the earth. Give it a go, and remember to get plenty of colour on those meatballs for maximum flavour!

To make 1 portion

2 spring onions

100g minced pork

1 garlic clove, crushed

1 mug of water

¼ mug of polenta

1 tsp chicken gravy granules

Handful of grated mature Cheddar cheese

Olive oil

Salt and pepper

To cook

Cut about 2cm from the green tops of the spring onions and finely chop. In a bowl, mix together the minced pork, chopped spring onion tops and garlic. Season well, form into 4 meatballs and pan-fry over a medium heat in a splash of oil.

While the meatballs are frying, bring the water to the boil in a saucepan, add a pinch of salt, then turn the heat down and slowly add the polenta while continuously stirring with a whisk. Continue to simmer over a very low heat for about 15 minutes until it forms a smooth, loose paste consistency.

When the meatballs are nicely browned all over and cooked through, slice the spring onions lengthways and add them to the pan (keep the meatballs in the pan), fry for a minute to soften, then add 60ml water and the gravy granules. Continue to cook for 1 minute, as you stir, to form a rich gravy.

Just before serving, remove the polenta from the heat and stir in the grated cheese. Pour onto a plate and top with the meatballs, spring onions and gravy.

CHICKEN FAJITAS

Over the past 10 years, fajitas have become a real family favourite in the UK. It just goes to show how a little spice and a bit of theatre can make even the simplest of ingredients the highlight of your food week. My One Pound Meals version of fajitas takes advantage of the fact that you can make your own tortilla wraps for pennies, and griddling the chicken and veg transforms the dish into an extra-healthy meal, too.

To make 1 portion

1 tsp paprika

1 tsp ground cumin

1 chicken thigh, de-boned

½ red onion, sliced

¼ green pepper, sliced

80g plain flour, plus extra for dusting (if needed)

50ml water

A few cherry tomatoes, chopped

2 tbsp crème fraîche

Olive oil

Salt and pepper

To cook

Mix the paprika and ground cumin in a bowl with a splash of olive oil and some salt and pepper, then coat your chicken in the mixture.

Cook the chicken in a preheated dry frying pan on both sides until the surface starts to char and the chicken is cooked through. Halfway through cooking, throw the onion and pepper into the pan too, turning them once they start to char.

While the chicken cooks, get started on the tortillas. Mix the flour and water in a bowl to form a dough. Tip the dough onto a worktop and knead for 5 minutes until smooth, adding more flour if the dough is too sticky, then divide in two and roll each piece into a 20cm circle using a rolling pin.

Preheat a dry frying pan over a high heat and cook the tortillas one at a time, for 2 minutes on each side, until they start to brown.

Slice your chicken into strips and arrange on the tortillas with the chargrilled vegetables. Add some chopped cherry tomatoes and dollop a tablespoonful of crème fraîche over each tortilla to complete your fajitas.

WARM GREEN BEAN SALAD

You have to try this warm salad. It's one of my all-time favourites. If you find salads a bit boring and think they're just for wimps, I guarantee this will change your mind. All those strong flavours from the mustard, the parmesan, the wilted onion and the cracked black pepper come together and are then magnified by the warmth of the beans to give the dish an extra kick.

To make 1 portion

Handful of green beans

1 tsp Dijon mustard

Small handful of flaked almonds

A few slices of onion

Small handful of parmesan shavings (use a potato peeler)

Olive oil

Salt and pepper

To cook

Bring a pan of salted water to the boil and cook the green beans for a few minutes until tender but still firm.

Drain the beans and, to save on washing up, return them to the same pan to be dressed.

Add the Dijon mustard, 4 teaspoons of olive oil, a pinch of salt, loads of freshly ground pepper, the flaked almonds, raw onion and most of the parmesan shavings. Give it a good stir until the onion starts to wilt slightly as it heats up.

Serve in a bowl and garnish with the remaining parmesan shavings.

PAELLA

This was a tricky recipe to create, and was one of the early eureka moments that helped shape the One Pound Meals style of cooking. This recipe shows how, with a bit of lateral thinking, a classic dish can be re-made by using ingredients in a slightly different way to achieve seemingly impossible results.

The main problem I faced with this dish was how to achieve a vibrant yellow rice colour without using saffron, the world's most expensive spice! Through experimentation, I found that by using a specific chicken stock cube that contained turmeric, and by using the paprika-infused oils from the pan-fried chorizo, everybody could now eat a delicious, vibrant-yellow paella for just £1 per serving!

To make 1 portion

25g soft chorizo, sliced

¼ onion, diced

¼ red pepper, sliced

100g long-grain rice

½ chicken stock cube

200ml water

40g frozen peas

50g cooked and peeled prawns

Lemon wedge (optional)

Olive oil

Salt and pepper

To cook

Pan-fry the chorizo in a splash of olive oil for 5 minutes over a medium heat until it starts to brown and the red paprika-infused oils have been released into the pan. Remove from the pan and set aside for later.

In the same pan, over a medium heat, fry the onion in the paprika-infused oil for 5 minutes until it starts to colour, then add the sliced pepper and rice, crumble in the stock cube and add 100ml of the water. Bring everything to the boil and simmer for 10 minutes, until most of the water has been absorbed by the rice. Add the rest of the water and continue to simmer until all the water has been absorbed and the rice is cooked. If you

find the rice needs longer, simply add a touch more water and continue to simmer until it has been absorbed.

Add the frozen peas, prawns and the pan-fried chorizo. Stir over a medium heat for 5 minutes until the peas are cooked, season to taste, then you are ready to serve it, with a wedge of lemon on the side.

STILTON-CRUSTED PORK LOIN

This amazingly simple stilton and breadcrumb topping is a real taste explosion! Consisting of just a small amount of cheese, a spring onion and some breadcrumbs, it manages to eke out every last ounce of flavour this dish could possibly give from so few ingredients. There's a veggie version on page 64.

To make 1 portion

1 potato, cut into small cubes

1 pork loin chop

20g stilton cheese, crumbled

Small handful of breadcrumbs (grated stale bread)

1 spring onion, chopped

Olive oil

Salt and pepper

To cook

Preheat your oven to 190°C/gas mark 5.

Put the cubed potatoes in an ovenproof dish, add a splash of olive oil and season with salt and pepper. Cook for 30 minutes in the oven until golden brown.

Season and pan-fry the pork chop over a medium heat, in a splash of olive oil, for about 6 minutes on each side.

Meanwhile, to make the topping, combine the crumbled stilton, breadcrumbs, and most of the spring onion in a bowl. Using your fingers, squash the ingredients together to form a paste.

Once the pork loin is cooked all the way through, spread the stilton topping over the top of the pork chop and cook under a preheated grill on high until the cheese is bubbling and starts to brown.

Serve with the crispy golden potatoes and a sprinkling of the remaining chopped spring onion.

MOROCCAN SPICED VEGETABLES, HUMMUS & FLATBREAD

Moroccan cuisine is renowned for taking the plainest vegetables and transforming them into exciting and vibrant dishes. Using Moroccan herbs and spices and slower cooking techniques, we can adopt this style of cooking and apply it to everyday supermarket veg to create our very own exciting and vibrant One Pound Meal.

To make 1 portion

¼ aubergine, roughly diced

½ red onion, roughly diced

½ courgette, roughly diced

1 carrot, roughly diced

1 tbsp harissa spice blend (or a mixture of paprika and ground cumin)

200g chickpeas (from a 400g tin), drained

1 garlic clove, crushed

40g plain flour

25ml cold water

Olive oil

Salt and pepper

To cook

Preheat your oven to 190°C/gas mark 5.

In an ovenproof dish, mix the aubergine, red onion, courgette and carrot with the harissa spice. Toss with a big glug of olive oil and season well. Roast in the oven for 40 minutes, until gooey and soft.

Meanwhile, prepare the hummus by microwaving the drained chickpeas in a bowl for 1 minute until soft. Using a potato masher, fork or blender, mash the chickpeas with the crushed garlic, plenty of salt and a splash of olive oil.

For the flatbread, mix the flour and water in a bowl to form a dough. Knead for 1 minute on the worktop then roll it out into a rough 20cm circle. Cook in a dry frying pan over a high heat for 2 minutes on each side, or until it starts to colour.

Serve the vegetables and hummus separately in bowls and use the flatbread to scoop it all up!

TOAD IN THE HOLE

This is a British comfort-food classic that will warm you up on the coldest of winter nights. It looks a lot more complicated than it actually is – just follow my steps and you'll be making huge Yorkshire puddings that rise spectacularly in the oven.

To make 1 portion

2 sausages

40g plain flour

1 large egg

60ml milk

A few baby carrots

A few broccoli florets

1 tsp gravy granules

Olive oil

Salt and pepper

To cook

Preheat your oven to 190°C/gas mark 5.

Cook the sausages in the oven on a baking tray for 15 minutes until lightly browned.

Add about 1cm of oil to a small ovenproof dish and heat it up for roughly 10 minutes in the oven until the oil is smoking hot.

Meanwhile, make the batter. Mix the flour, egg and milk in a bowl with a pinch of salt then, very carefully, remove the dish from the oven and add the sausages, carrots and broccoli. Pour in the batter and return it immediately to the oven. Do not open the oven door for at least 15 minutes, and after about 20 minutes the batter should have risen perfectly and will be a lovely golden brown colour.

Mix the gravy granules with some boiling water (according to the packet instructions) and serve with your toad in the hole.

HAM & CHEESE CRÊPES

There's a guy near me who sells these for £5 each, and on Sundays the queue is a mile long! So, I just couldn't resist the challenge, and I created my own super-easy and delicious version for a tenth of the price. As with a lot of my One Pound Meals, you can use these recipes as templates and add whatever ingredients you may have in the fridge. My favourite filling is ham and cheese, but why not try goats' cheese and spinach? Or, go for the insanely popular chocolate-spread filling? Give yourself a treat every Sunday with these One Pound Meals crêpes.

To make 1 portion (2 crêpes)

50g plain flour

1 egg

150ml milk

Handful of grated cheese

1 slice of ham

Olive oil

Salt and pepper

To cook

In a bowl or jug, whisk together the flour, egg and milk with a pinch of salt.

Preheat a large frying pan over a medium-high heat. Very lightly grease it with oil, then pour half the crêpe mixture into the pan, tilting it to ensure the batter spreads evenly to the edges of the pan.

After about 1 minute, check the underside is cooked and starting to turn golden brown, then carefully flip the crêpe to cook the other side.

While the other side is cooking, add half the cheese and ham to one half of the crêpe and, as the cheese starts to melt, fold the crêpe in half. Cook for a little longer then fold in half again, and then once more. Repeat with the rest of the crêpe mixture and filling to make a second crêpe.

...and, for the authentic crêpe-van feel, wrap the crêpes into neat triangles using greaseproof paper.

CHICKEN EN CROUTE

The French have a way of elevating the most standard of ingredients into a fun and impressive centrepiece to a meal. When you 'en croute' this chicken thigh, you will be transforming it into your very own showpiece!

To make 1 portion

1 chicken thigh, skin removed and de-boned

Handful of feta cheese, crumbled

A few sun-dried tomatoes, diced

Sheet of puff pastry

Olive oil

Salt and pepper

To cook

Preheat your oven to 190°C/gas mark 5.

Season and pan-fry the chicken thigh in a splash of olive oil over a medium heat for 8 minutes on each side, until cooked through, then set aside.

Meanwhile, combine the feta with the sun-dried tomatoes in a bowl.

Cut a square of puff pastry (large enough to wrap the chicken with), pile the feta and tomato mixture in the middle, top with the cooked and cooled chicken thigh, then carefully enclose the chicken by wrapping the pastry around it and tucking the pastry edges underneath so it has a smooth top.

Trim the excess pastry and lightly score a criss-cross pattern on the top. Place on a non-stick baking tray and bake for 20 minutes until golden brown.

I like to cut my chicken 'en croute' at an angle with a bread knife before serving, to show off the centre.

AUBERGINE DAL & CHAPATI

This dal dish is definitely at the top of my list of economical meals. Without a doubt, the super-cheap lentils pack a flavour punch much more powerful than their low price tag would suggest. I also add cubes of gorgeous, sticky, oven-roasted, curried aubergine that will keep even the most vocal of carnivores quiet.

To make 1 portion

¼ aubergine, cut into chunky cubes

3 tsp curry powder

¼ onion, finely diced

1 garlic clove, sliced

2 handfuls of red lentils (approx. 80g)

375ml water

40g wholemeal flour, plus extra if necessary

Vegetable oil (or olive oil)

Salt and pepper

To cook

Preheat your oven to 190°C/gas mark 5.

Put the aubergine cubes in an ovenproof dish. Add a splash of vegetable oil and a teaspoon of the curry powder, then mix well to evenly coat the aubergine.

Slowly roast the aubergine in the oven for 30 minutes until golden brown, with a gorgeous gooey and sticky texture.

Meanwhile, fry the onion in a splash of vegetable oil over a medium heat. After a few minutes, add the garlic and continue to fry for a few more minutes until the garlic is just about starting to brown. At this point, add the remaining curry powder, lentils and 350ml of the water.

Bring the lentils to the boil and simmer gently over a low heat for 20 minutes, or until the lentils are fully cooked and have a lovely rich, thick consistency.

While the lentils are simmering and the aubergine is roasting, make your chapati dough. In a bowl, mix the wholemeal flour, the remaining 25ml water and a pinch of salt to form a dough. Tip the dough onto the worktop and knead for 5 minutes, adding more flour if the dough is too sticky, then roll it into a 20cm circle using a rolling pin.

Preheat a dry frying pan over a high heat and cook the chapati for 2 minutes on each side, or until toasted golden brown spots start appearing.

Season the dal with salt, add the aubergine cubes, and serve with the warm chapati on the side.

PORK LOIN & CREAMY MUSHROOM PAPPARDELLE

Pasta is amazingly versatile, economical and delicious, and a great One Pound Meals ingredient. To make this extra-wide pappardelle, I used lasagne sheets and cut them into strips – it's much cheaper and looks a lot cooler! Then, because I wanted to keep the pork chop separate, I used the pasta as more of a side dish. Finally, all it needed was a lovely creamy mushroom sauce to tie the dish together.

To make 1 portion

4 dried lasagne sheets

1 pork loin chop

Handful of mushrooms (approx. 50g), chopped

1 garlic clove, chopped

50ml single cream

Olive oil

Salt and pepper

To cook

Bring a pan of salted water to the boil and cook the lasagne sheets until al dente, then drain, drizzle with olive oil and cut into wide strips.

Season and pan-fry the pork loin chop over a medium heat, in a splash of olive oil, for about 7 minutes on each side until cooked through.

Remove the pork from the pan then fry the mushrooms in another splash of olive oil until nicely golden brown. Add the chopped garlic and continue to fry for a minute then add the cream.

Let the cream reduce for a minute then, when the sauce is thickened, remove from the heat and serve the pork chop on a bed of the pasta, topped with the creamy mushroom sauce.

ROAST CHICKEN BALLOTINE & POTATOES

This recipe is definitely the most fiddly dish in the book, but it really shows how with a bit of effort and a push in the right direction, the humblest of ingredients can be turned into something quite spectacular. When you really need to impress someone, turn to this page – this dish won't let you down.

I've also used this technique in my Ultimate £1 Roast (see page 144) and Christmas Dinner (see page 160), so once you've mastered it, you'll have the confidence to make the others.

To make 1 portion

1 mushroom, diced

1 garlic clove, diced

Handful of spinach

3 rashers of smoked streaky bacon

1 chicken leg, de-boned and skin on

A few small potatoes, halved

Olive oil

Salt and pepper

To cook

First, make the stuffing by pan-frying the mushroom, garlic and most of the spinach over a medium heat with a splash of olive oil, until the mushroom is cooked and the spinach wilted. Season well, then allow to cool while you prepare the chicken.

Lay the bacon rashers next to each other on a sheet of tin foil to form a neat rectangle, then lay the chicken leg on top (skin-side down). Place a line of stuffing across the middle of the chicken. Wrap everything into a neat cylinder and twist each end of the foil to tighten it. Wrap 4 pieces of butcher's string around the cylinder, just tight enough to create ridges in the surface of the foil.

Poach the chicken in boiling water for 25 minutes, then cool under cold running water and refrigerate for a minimum of 30 minutes (you can do this the night before).

Peel the foil off the chicken (don't remove the string) and pan-fry in a splash of olive oil over a medium heat for about 15 minutes, turning it frequently using tongs to get a nice colour on the bacon (make sure the chicken is hot throughout).

Meanwhile, boil the potatoes in a pan of salted water until cooked. Drain and pan-fry the potatoes for about 5 minutes over a high heat with a splash of olive oil and a pinch of salt and pepper. Remove from the heat, immediately stir in the rest of the spinach and allow it to wilt.

Serve the chicken ballotine on a bed of potatoes and enjoy your well-earned £1 feast.

LAMB MOUSSAKA STACK

This is a fun, modern interpretation of a moussaka. It's slightly unusual – sort of like a moussaka toasted cheese sandwich – but that's what makes it jump out of the page at you. By keeping food fun, you'll be motivated to give new things a try, and this recipe is much simpler than it looks. So have a go, then post it on Instagram to see what your friends think. There's a vegetarian version on page 28.

To make 1 portion

¼ red onion, diced

75g minced lamb

1 garlic clove, sliced

1 tsp dried oregano, plus extra to garnish

100g chopped tomatoes (from a 400g tin)

1 tsp butter

1 tsp plain flour

50ml milk

Handful of grated mature Cheddar cheese

1 egg, beaten

2 x 1cm-thick slices of aubergine, cut lengthways

Olive oil

Salt and pepper

To cook

Preheat your oven to 190°C/gas mark 5.

Fry the onion and minced lamb in a pan over a medium heat in a splash of olive oil, seasoning it well, until the lamb turns a lovely golden brown.

Add the garlic and the oregano, fry for a few minutes, then add the chopped tomatoes. Simmer gently for 10 minutes until the tomatoes break down and the sauce thickens.

Meanwhile, to make the cheesy topping, melt the butter in a saucepan over a medium heat then stir in the flour. Slowly whisk in the milk to create a thick sauce, remove from the heat and stir in the grated cheese. Mix in half the beaten egg (keep the rest of the beaten egg in the fridge for another recipe).

Assemble the moussaka by laying a slice of aubergine on a baking tray, spooning over the lamb mince, sandwiching the filling with the second slice of aubergine and topping the whole thing with the thick cheesy sauce.

Cook in the oven for about 20 minutes, or until the topping is golden brown, then scatter with extra oregano to serve.

STUFFED RED PEPPER

This recipe is a super-easy and speedy way to make a delicious vegetarian classic. By oven-roasting this couscous-filled pepper, the top will become crispy and contrast nicely with the soft and salty feta cheese.

To make 1 portion

2 spring onions, roughly chopped

Handful of couscous

1 red pepper

40g feta, cubed

Olive oil

Salt and pepper

To cook

Preheat your oven to 190°C/gas mark 5.

Gently fry the spring onions over a medium heat in a splash of olive oil. Just before they start to colour, add the couscous and a splash of water (about 20ml). Remove from the heat and allow to rest while you halve and de-seed the pepper. After 5 minutes the couscous will have doubled in size. Add the cubed feta to the couscous, then stuff the pepper halves and season.

Cook the stuffed peppers in the oven on a baking tray for 20 minutes, or until the pepper is cooked, then serve.

CHICKEN PANZANELLA TRAY BAKE

I love a traditional panzanella salad. My favourite part is the stale bread, which soaks up all the juices from the tomatoes and the balsamic vinegar. So, with this recipe, I wanted to take it one step further and roast the whole thing with chicken so that the bread soaks up all the roasting juices, too. This recipe is one of my go-to ways to use up stale bread.

To make 1 portion

2 chicken drumsticks

A few small tomatoes

¼ yellow pepper, roughly chopped

½ red onion, roughly chopped

1 tbsp balsamic vinegar

Chunks of stale bread

Olive oil

Salt and pepper

To cook

Preheat your oven to 190°C/gas mark 5.

To make the finished dish look extra lovely on the plate, deeply score the drumsticks to the bone in the middle and at the narrow end. Season with salt and pepper and drizzle with olive oil, then roast in the oven on a baking tray for about 15 minutes.

Remove the tray from the oven and add the tomatoes, pepper and onion. Season well and drizzle with more olive oil and the balsamic vinegar. Cook in the oven for a further 25 minutes, throwing in the bread about halfway through, until the chicken is golden brown and cooked through.

Mop up all the juices with the toasted bread and enjoy your tangy oven-roasted chicken panzanella salad.

HUEVOS CON CHORIZO

This is a lovely brunch dish that will put a smile on your face. It has a slight kick to it with the spicy chorizo, the potatoes are drenched with that gorgeous paprika-infused oil, and it's all topped off with a runny egg and sweet caramelised peppers. This is how to do brunch with big, bold flavours.

To make I portion

A handful of small potatoes, halved

Small handful of roughly diced cooking chorizo

¼ red pepper, sliced

1 egg

Olive oil

Salt and pepper

To cook

Boil the new potatoes in a pan of salted water until cooked all the way through, then drain.

Pan-fry the chorizo in a splash of olive oil over a medium heat. As the chorizo starts to colour, add the sliced pepper and potatoes. Continue to fry until the pepper and potatoes have coloured nicely, season, then crack the egg on top and finish under the grill.

I like to serve this straight from the pan with a chunk of bread to mop up the egg yolk and that amazing paprika-infused oil.

LASAGNE

Here's a One Pound Meals favourite! Lasagne is a real crowd-pleaser and is perfect for scaling up to feed a whole group of friends and family. This is a dish that you can be proud to boast was made entirely from scratch, even the béchamel sauce!

To make 1 portion

¼ onion, diced

125g minced beef

1 garlic clove, sliced

200g chopped tomatoes (from a 400g tin)

1 tsp butter

1 tsp plain flour

150ml milk

45g mature Cheddar cheese, grated

2 dried lasagne sheets

Olive oil

Salt and pepper

To cook

Preheat your oven to 190°C/gas mark 5.

Pan-fry the diced onion over a medium heat with a splash of olive oil for 5 minutes until soft, then add the minced beef, season with salt and pepper and continue to fry until the meat is nicely browned. Add the garlic and fry for a further 1–2 minutes, then add the tomatoes. Simmer over a low heat for 10 minutes while you make the béchamel sauce.

Melt the butter in a saucepan over a medium heat, then add the flour. Stir to form a paste, then add the milk very slowly while continuing to stir until you have a thick sauce. Remove from the heat and stir in a handful of the grated cheese to finish the sauce.

In an ovenproof dish, layer half of your filling, then a sheet of pasta and half of your béchamel sauce. Repeat the layering process and top with the rest of the cheese to create that signature caramelised lasagne topping.

Cook in the oven for 25 minutes, until the lasagne has a perfectly golden top.

CHICKEN TIKKA MASALA

Chicken Tikka Masala is the nation's favourite dish, so I simply had to take the One Pound Meals challenge and recreate it for under a quid. And it was a huge success! By griddling marinated chicken thighs, I managed to get that charred tandoor tikka effect. Then, by reducing tinned tomatoes and enriching them with cream, the sauce now has that local takeaway authenticity that a ready-meal just can't provide.

To make 1 portion

½ mug of basmati rice

1 mug of water

1 chicken thigh, de-boned

3 tsp tandoori curry powder

¼ onion, sliced

200g chopped tomatoes (from a 400g tin)

50ml single cream

Olive oil

Salt and pepper

To cook

Put the rice and water in a saucepan, bring to the boil and simmer gently, with the lid on, for about 7 minutes. When all the water has been absorbed, remove from the heat and set aside until ready to serve.

Meanwhile, in a bowl, coat the chicken in 1 teaspoon of the tandoori curry powder and a splash of oil. Preheat a griddle pan (or frying pan) until hot, then chargrill your chicken skin-side down for 7 minutes, then a further 7 minutes on the other side, until cooked through.

While the chicken is cooking, gently fry the onion in a separate pan with a splash of oil over a medium heat. When softened, add the tomatoes and the remaining curry powder and simmer for 5 minutes until reduced a little. Next, add the cream and continue to simmer for a few minutes until you reach the desired takeaway masala sauce consistency.

Cut your griddled chicken into cubes and stir them into the sauce to create your chicken tikka masala. Serve with the rice and enjoy on a Friday night with a cold beer!

QUICHE LORRAINE

Making quiche is much easier than it looks: the pastry is just made of flour, butter and water, and the filling is pretty simple, too. Here I have used the classic quiche lorraine filling of bacon, onion and Cheddar cheese, but you can use this One Pound Meals template to create any quiche your mind can imagine, or use up any leftover ingredients you may have lying around. One big advantage of quiches is that the ingredients are cooked and then chilled, so a quiche will last for days in the fridge. If you like making pastry, see my Cornish Pasty on page 198.

To make 1 portion

100g plain flour, plus extra for dusting

50g chilled butter

25ml cold water

1 red onion, sliced

4 smoked bacon rashers, chopped

100ml milk

2 eggs

50g mature Cheddar cheese, grated

Olive oil

Salt and pepper

To cook

Preheat your oven to 190°C/gas mark 5.

Mix the flour and butter in a bowl by gently rubbing them together using your fingertips until the mixture resembles damp sand. Add the water and gently knead to form a dough. Gently roll out the dough on a floured worktop to about the thickness of a £1 coin and use it to line a 15cm round ovenproof dish.

Prick the base all over with a fork and bake it empty in the oven for 10 minutes.

Meanwhile, make the filling. Start by frying the onion in a pan with a splash of olive oil until softened, then add the bacon and continue to cook until it starts to go crispy. Remove from the heat and allow to cool a bit.

In a bowl or jug, mix the milk, eggs and cheese, then add the bacon and onion, and season with salt and pepper.

Pour the mixture into the pre-baked pastry shell and cook for 20 minutes in the oven until the top is a delicious golden brown colour.

LEEK, POTATO & STILTON SOUP

This hearty soup is a bonafide main course in a bowl. The sautéed leeks coupled with the stilton give the dish a great depth of flavour, and the potatoes make it extra filling, ensuring you get that comforting glow. Enjoy with a chunk of rustic bread to mop up every last drop.

To make I portion

½ leek, chopped

Handful of new potatoes, quartered

250ml water

1 vegetable stock cube

20g stilton cheese, crumbled

Olive oil

Salt and pepper

To cook

Fry the chopped leek with a splash of olive oil in a saucepan over a medium heat for 5 minutes, until softened, then add some ground black pepper.

Add the potatoes and water, crumble in the stock cube, then simmer for 15 minutes until the potatoes are soft and cooked through.

Next, add the contents of the pan to a blender but first set aside a few cooked potatoes and leeks to add at the end – this will provide a nice contrasting texture.

Add some of the crumbled stilton then blend the mixture to create a lovely velvety soup. Taste and season if required (the stilton is quite salty). Pour the soup into a bowl, sprinkle over the remaining stilton, and add the reserved chunks of potato and leek to create the final dish. Serve with a chunk of crusty bread and enjoy on a cold winter's day.

CHICKEN STEW & DUMPLINGS

As soon as winter hits, you'll be looking for warming dishes, like this chicken stew with dumplings, to give you that comforting food hug. These dumplings, with their doughy fluffy centres, go lovely and crisp in the oven, and are perfect for mopping up this rich chicken gravy.

To make 1 portion

1 chicken thigh, de-boned

1 onion, roughly chopped

A few baby carrots (or chunky diced carrots)

A few small potatoes, roughly diced

1 tsp plain flour

1 chicken stock cube

250ml water

80g self-raising flour

1 tsp butter

Olive oil

Salt and pepper

To cook

Preheat your oven to 190°C/gas mark 5.

Season your chicken thigh, then gently fry it skin-side down in a small casserole dish with a splash of olive oil. When the chicken is nicely coloured on both sides, remove from the pan and add the onion. Deglaze the base of the dish, using the onion pieces to scrape off the chickeny goodness. Once the onion has softened and is starting to brown, add the carrots and potatoes. Cook for a couple of minutes while you chop the pan-fried chicken into several chunky pieces, return the chicken to the dish, season well, then stir in the flour. Crumble in the stock cube and stir in the water. Remove from the heat and set aside while you make the dumplings.

To make the dumplings, grab a bowl and simply mix the flour with the butter by crumbling it between your fingertips until it has the texture of damp sand. Season with salt and pepper and then – by just adding a splash of cold water – the mixture will come together like a dough. Shape the dough into 2 balls.

Top the stew with the dumpling balls, transfer to the oven and cook for about 30 minutes, until the dumplings are golden brown.

CHINESE GLAZED PORK

Pork belly is a great economical cut of meat that, with a bit of care and attention, can be transformed into wonderfully succulent Chinese glazed pork. By starting with a slow simmer, the pork takes on a beautiful extra-soft texture that contrasts perfectly with its quick pan-fried crisp and sticky outer glaze. Throw in some egg-fried rice and you've got a fabulous Chinese meal for under £1.

To make 1 portion

2 pork belly slices

½ mug of long-grain rice

1 mug of water

Sesame oil

1 egg

1 spring onion, sliced

1 tbsp honey

1 tsp Chinese 5-spice

Vegetable oil

Salt and pepper

To cook

Cook the pork belly slices in a saucepan of water over a low heat, covered, for 1½ hours.

Meanwhile, in a separate saucepan, bring the water and rice to the boil, cover and simmer gently. When the rice is cooked and has absorbed all the water, tip it into a bowl and allow to cool to room temperature (or refrigerate).

When the pork is cooked and drained, and the rice is cold, heat a wok (or large saucepan) over a high heat and add a splash of sesame oil along with the rice. As the rice starts to fry – keep on stirring so that it doesn't burn on the bottom – scoop everything to one side of the pan and crack the egg into the empty side. Start to fry the egg and, once it is half cooked, scramble it with a wooden spoon and mix it in with the rice. Add the spring onion (keeping a little to garnish) and another splash of sesame oil then remove from the heat.

Meanwhile, pan-fry the pork belly with a splash of vegetable oil until the pork starts to colour. At this point, add the honey, Chinese 5-spice and a pinch of salt and pepper. Continue to fry for a minute and evenly coat the pork belly with the honey glaze. When the glaze turns dark brown, remove from the pan and serve the pork with the egg-fried rice and the reserved spring onion.

DIJON CHICKEN

This dish encapsulates the One Pound Meals philosophy by making your life easy. You just need one pan, it is simple to make, and – with a quick cheat of softening the potatoes in a microwave – it is super speedy. But, above all, it is absolutely delicious!

To make 1 portion

1 chicken thigh, de-boned

4 charlotte potatoes, halved

1 spring onion, roughly chopped

2 mushrooms, sliced

½ chicken stock cube

50ml cold water

1 tsp Dijon mustard

Olive oil

Salt and pepper

To cook

Season and pan-fry the chicken skin-side down over a medium heat in a splash of olive oil.

Meanwhile, soften the potatoes in a microwave for 1 minute (or boil for 5 minutes).

After about 5 minutes, or when the chicken skin is nicely browned, turn it over and continue to fry for another 5 minutes. When the chicken is almost cooked, add the spring onion, mushrooms and potatoes to the pan and continue to fry for a few more minutes until everything is cooked. At this point, crumble in the stock cube, add the water and simmer for a few minutes before adding the Dijon mustard. Stir and continue to simmer for a couple of minutes, reducing the sauce slightly, then serve.

SCOTCH EGGS

Ever wondered how Scotch eggs are actually made? Well, it's not as difficult as you'd think, so impress your friends with these fun treats and, if you manage to get a runny yolk, then you know you've nailed it!

To make 2 Scotch eggs

3 eggs

1 tbsp plain flour

Big handful of breadcrumbs (grated stale bread)

200g minced pork

Sunflower oil

Salt and pepper

To cook

Bring a saucepan of water to the boil and cook 2 of the eggs for exactly 7 minutes, then cool them quickly under cold running water to stop the cooking process.

Place the flour and some seasoning in one bowl, beat the third egg in another bowl, and put the breadcrumbs and some seasoning in a third bowl.

Mix the minced pork in a bowl with some salt and pepper.

Peel the 2 cooked and cooled eggs and wrap them with the minced pork. Roll them in the flour, then the beaten egg, then coat in the breadcrumbs.

Turn on the deep-fat fryer to pre-heat, or heat some sunflower oil in a saucepan (about half-full). Fry the Scotch eggs for about 10 minutes, until golden brown and the meat is cooked through.

PORK STROGANOFF

This dish has a lovely kick to it, thanks to the addition of paprika. It's a speedy dish to prepare and makes a great evening meal for busy people with adventurous tastes.

To make 1 portion

½ mug of brown rice

1 mug of water

¼ onion, diced

1 garlic clove, sliced

1 pork loin chop (approx. 100g), cut into strips

Handful of mushrooms, sliced

1 tsp paprika

100ml single cream

Handful of spinach

Olive oil

Salt and pepper

To cook

Put the rice and water in a saucepan, bring to the boil, cover, then simmer gently for about 10 minutes, or until all the water has been absorbed and the rice is cooked.

While the rice is cooking, gently pan-fry the onion in a splash of olive oil over a medium heat. After a few minutes, add the garlic and then the strips of pork. Season and continue to cook for a few minutes. When the pork is starting to brown, add the mushrooms and paprika and continue to fry until the pork is cooked through.

To finish the dish, add the cream and simmer for a few minutes until the sauce thickens slightly, then stir in the spinach and, once it has wilted, serve with the rice.

ULTIMATE £1 BURGER

This burger will beat any high-street competition. Fully loaded with salad, mature Cheddar, smoked bacon and even giant crispy onion rings, and all for under £1, THIS is the king of burgers!

To make I portion

½ red onion

125g minced beef

20g self-raising flour

25ml cold water

1 rasher of smoked streaky bacon

10g mature Cheddar cheese, grated

A few lettuce leaves

A few slices of tomato

1 bun

Olive oil

Salt and pepper

To cook

Firstly, prepare the onion in 3 different ways: you need 3 chunky rings for the onion rings, a few thin slices for the salad in the burger, and the rest very finely chopped for the burger.

In a bowl, mix the minced beef with the finely chopped onion, season well and form into a burger shape. Start frying it in a pan over a medium heat with a splash of olive oil.

Meanwhile, to make the onion rings, preheat a small saucepan of oil about 2cm deep, or switch on a deep-fat fryer. In a bowl, mix the self-raising flour with the water, coat a chunky ring of onion and fry for 3 minutes until golden brown. Repeat with the two remaining chunky rings.

When the burger is nicely coloured and cooked through, remove from the pan and fry the bacon until crispy. Add the grated cheese to the top of the burger and melt it under the grill.

Assemble your ultimate burger in the bun with lettuce, thin slices of onion, tomato, the burger with melted cheese, bacon, and then top with the onion rings.

CLUB SANDWICH

Top hotels across the world are judged on this one dish alone. There are even league tables ranking hotels purely on the quality of their club sandwiches. So, let's try and make the best club sandwich in the world for just £1. Firstly, the bread will make or break your sandwich, so for the most decadent club sandwich, you must always toast your bread in a frying pan or on a griddle using a tiny bit of olive oil, salt and pepper. Without this step, there is no way your bread will hold this many ingredients. With these firm foundations, just follow this recipe and everything else will fall into place.

To make 1 portion

2 chicken thighs, skin on and de-boned

3 rashers of smoked streaky bacon

3 slices of bread

A few Little Gem lettuce leaves

1 tomato, sliced

Mayo

Olive oil

Salt and pepper

To cook

Pan-fry the chicken thighs skin-side down over a medium heat with a splash of olive oil for 7 minutes, then flip and fry for a further 7 minutes, until golden brown and cooked through. Remove from the pan to rest while you fry the bacon.

Meanwhile, for the bread, lightly drizzle some olive oil on each side, season with salt and pepper, and fry over a medium heat in a frying pan or on a griddle until golden brown.

Arrange your sandwich by placing one slice of bread on a board, adding a layer of lettuce, then tomato, a tiny bit of cracked black pepper, the chicken thighs and a generous dollop of mayo. Then, add the middle slice of bread and repeat the layers, this time adding the bacon. Then finish the dish with the third slice of bread, securing it with a wooden skewer to stop it toppling over.

SMOKED MACKEREL FISH CAKE & DIJON SAUCE

My Smoked Mackerel Fish Cake & Dijon Sauce is one of the best One Pound Meals to impress your guests with at a dinner party. The rich smoky flavours of the smoked mackerel are absorbed by the potato to create a sophisticated, intense flavour that complements the Dijon sauce.

To make 1 portion

1 medium potato, peeled and quartered

50g smoked mackerel

1 tbsp plain flour, plus 1 tsp

1 egg, beaten

Handful of breadcrumbs (grated stale bread)

1 tsp butter

50ml milk

2 tsp Dijon mustard

Handful of spinach

Olive oil or vegetable oil

Salt and pepper

To cook

Cook the potato quarters in salted boiling water until soft enough to pierce with a fork, then drain and mash. Once the mash cools down a bit, shred the smoked mackerel with your fingertips or a fork and combine it with the mashed potato.

Season well with salt and pepper and form into a flat circular shape either by hand or using something like an egg ring to create a neater shape. To help keep the shape, refrigerate for 30 minutes until chilled all the way through.

Place the flour and some seasoning in one bowl, the beaten egg in another bowl, and the breadcrumbs and some seasoning in a third bowl. Dust the chilled fish cake with the seasoned flour, dip it in the beaten egg and cover in seasoned breadcrumbs.

Pan-fry the fish cake over a medium heat in plenty of olive oil, making sure to evenly brown all sides, or deep-fry in vegetable oil until golden brown.

While the fish cake is cooking, make the sauce by melting the butter in a pan over a medium heat, adding the teaspoon of flour, then slowly whisking in the milk. As the sauce starts to come together, season and stir in the Dijon mustard.

To serve, pour the sauce into a shallow bowl, place the spinach in the middle and rest the fish cake on top.

KALE & FRIED POLENTA STACK

Here is something special for vegetarians. Sometimes it's nice to go a little overboard with the presentation and push the boat out. This dish has so many of my favourite earthy flavours, so make sure you add loads of cracked black pepper – it can definitely handle it. And I have added some cheese to the polenta to make it even more luxurious!

To make 1 portion

1 mug of water

¼ mug of polenta

Small handful of mature Cheddar cheese, grated

Handful of mushrooms, sliced

1 garlic clove, sliced

Handful of kale

1 tbsp crème fraîche

Olive oil

Salt and pepper

To cook

Lightly salt the water, bring it to the boil in a saucepan and turn the heat down, then slowly add the polenta while stirring with a whisk.

After about 10 minutes the polenta will have the consistency of mashed potato and will be fully cooked. Remove from the heat and stir in the grated cheese. Empty into a small container that's big enough to allow you to cut 2 nice circular pieces once the polenta has set. Leave to set at room temperature for 30 minutes (or in the fridge overnight), then cut out 2 shapes using the rim of a wine glass.

Fry the polenta discs over a medium heat in a splash of oil and flip them every so often until they start to colour. Watch out as they will be very fragile, so gently shake the pan every so often to make sure they don't stick.

Meanwhile, in a separate frying pan, fry the mushrooms in a splash of olive oil over a medium heat. After a few minutes, throw in the garlic and kale. Keep stirring for a few minutes until the kale starts to wilt. Season with a bit of salt and lots of pepper, then add the crème fraîche. Mix it all together and carefully arrange the polenta, mushrooms and kale into a two-storey tower.

MUSHROOM RISOTTO

Risotto is a very important dish for One Pound Meals. It illustrates perfectly how, with a bit of love and care, you can elevate a simple ingredient such as rice into a delicious dish with far more complex flavours and textures. Once you have learnt how to make it, you'll find it has an almost endless number of variations (including my Butternut Squash Risotto on page 32). Risotto is perfect for using up small amounts of leftovers that need to be bulked out into a main meal. So, armed with risotto in your repertoire of dishes, you need never be daunted by leftovers again!

To make 1 portion

¼ onion, diced

Handful of Arborio risotto rice (approx. 125g)

500ml boiling water

1 stock cube

100g mushrooms, sliced

Handful of grated parmesan (approx. 10g)

Olive oil

Salt and pepper

To cook

Start by filling a kettle and boiling some water.

Pan-fry the diced onion in a splash of olive oil over a medium heat. After 5 minutes, when the onion is slightly translucent in colour but before it starts to brown, add the rice and season with a pinch of salt and pepper.

Add 100ml of the hot water from the pre-boiled kettle and crumble in the stock cube. Stir the rice over a medium heat as the stock cube dissolves.

After a couple of minutes, the rice will have absorbed most of the water. At this point add another 100ml of hot water from the kettle and continue stirring.

Keep adding hot water in small amounts as you continue to stir the risotto, and you will notice the rice starts to get creamier and creamier.

Meanwhile, in a separate pan, fry the mushrooms in a splash of olive oil over a medium heat for 10 minutes, along with some salt and pepper, until they are golden brown in colour, then remove from the heat and set to one side.

After about 20 minutes of adding water and stirring the rice, give it a taste and, once you have that perfect firm but creamy texture, remove from the heat.

Stir most of the grated parmesan and all the sautéed mushrooms into the rice.

Serve scattered with the rest of the parmesan, and enjoy!

FETA TORTELLINI PUTTANESCA

This is rustic cooking at its finest: simple ingredients, simple flavours and simple presentation. While not a typical Italian ingredient, feta works so well with the oregano and olives, creating a sort of hybrid Italian-Greek dish. Once you have learned to make your own filled pasta, start experimenting with your own flavour combinations, too – this is a great way to use up leftover ingredients and have fun in the kitchen (have a look at the next two recipes). You'll have more than enough dough, so why not freeze the leftover dough for another day.

To make 1 portion

100g Italian '00' pasta flour, plus extra for dusting

1 egg

50g feta cheese

1 tsp dried oregano

¼ onion, sliced

1 garlic clove, sliced

200g chopped tomatoes (from a 400g tin)

Handful of black pitted olives

Olive oil

Salt and pepper

To cook

In a bowl, mix the flour with the egg to form a dough. Knead it on a floured worktop for 5 minutes until you have a smooth dough, wrap it in cling film and allow to rest for 20 minutes in the fridge.

To make it easier to work with, cut the dough in half.

Lightly dust half of the dough with flour (freeze the other half, or make more tortellini! Double the filling quantities if you use all the dough) and roll it out as thinly as you possibly can with a rolling pin (or a pasta rolling machine).

Next, using the rim of a wine glass, cut out as many circles of pasta as you can and lay them on the worktop ready for filling.

Crumble the feta cheese onto a small plate and sprinkle over a pinch of the oregano.

Dip a fingertip in water and run it around half the edge of a pasta circle. Place a compact, almond-sized piece of the feta filling in the centre and fold the circle in half. Make sure there is no air trapped inside, then gently press the edges together to form a seal. Next, bring the two ends of the semi-circle together while slightly pushing the filling upwards, pull it tight and pinch the ends together to make them stick. This will create a flower effect with the filling in the centre and the edges wrapped around it like petals. Repeat with the rest of the pasta and most of the filling (leave some to sprinkle over the finished dish).

There are many different ways to wrap tortellini, so if you want an easier way, use squares of pasta instead of circles and just wrap them like sweets

by twisting the ends. But don't forget to use some water to create the seal.

Get a saucepan of salted water on the boil for the pasta, and start making the sauce.

Fry the onion over a medium heat in a splash of olive oil until it starts to colour, then add the garlic and fry for a few more minutes. Add the chopped tomatoes, olives and a pinch of the oregano. Simmer to thicken the sauce slightly and season with salt and plenty of pepper.

Boil the pasta for 2 minutes, while the sauce is simmering, then drain and add it to the sauce. Mix everything together and serve with a generous glug of olive oil, more pepper and the leftover pasta filling crumbled on top.

PRAWN WONTON SOUP

This recipe shows how, with a bit of imagination, techniques learnt from different styles of cooking can be applied in ways you wouldn't expect. Here, using a simple Italian technique for making tortellini, you can create these delicate little prawn wontons. You'll have double the quantity of dough you need, so why not freeze the leftover dough for another day. Or try the Tortellini (see page 132) or Gyoza (see page 138).

To make 1 portion

100g Italian '00' pasta flour, plus extra
  for dusting

1 egg

4 cooked and peeled prawns

1 spring onion, sliced

Sesame oil

Soy sauce

400ml water

1 chicken stock cube

½ sheet of dried noodles (approx. 40g)

¼ pak choi

To cook

In a bowl, mix the flour with the egg to form a dough. Knead it on a floured worktop for 5 minutes until smooth, wrap it in cling film and allow to rest for 20 minutes in the fridge.

While the dough is resting, very finely chop the prawns and a quarter of the sliced spring onion. Transfer to a bowl, add a splash of sesame oil and a splash of soy sauce, then mash with the back of a fork to mix everything together.

To make it easier to work with, cut the dough in half. Lightly dust half of the dough with flour (freeze the other half, or make more wontons! Double the filling quantities if you use all the dough), and roll it out as thinly as you possibly can with a rolling pin (or a pasta rolling machine). Using the rim of a wine glass, cut out about 7 circles and lay them on the worktop.

Dip a fingertip in water and run it around half the edge of a pasta circle. Spoon an almond-sized amount of the prawn filling into the centre and fold the circle in half. Make sure there is no air trapped inside, then gently press the edges together to seal.

Leave your wontons as semi-circles or create that classic compact wonton shape by folding the two furthest edges of the semi-circle together. Repeat with the rest of the pasta circles and filling.

Bring the water to the boil in a saucepan over a medium heat with the remaining spring onion, and crumble in the stock cube. Add the noodles and cook for 2 minutes, then add the pak choi. Cook for a further 2 minutes, then add the wontons. Simmer for 2 minutes until the noodles are cooked, add a splash of soy sauce, then serve in a bowl with a ladle of the cooking stock.

PORK & SPRING ONION GYOZA

With One Pound Meals, you don't need to be scared of seemingly complicated dishes like pork gyoza. I've taken some huge shortcuts for you so now, if you break it down, this recipe is simply some easy pasta dough filled with pork mince. Have a look at the previous two recipes for more ideas.

To make 1 portion

100g Italian '00' pasta flour, plus extra for dusting

1 egg

30g minced pork

1 spring onion, finely diced

1 garlic clove, crushed

Sesame oil

Soy sauce

Salt and pepper

To cook

In a bowl, mix the flour with the egg to form a dough. Knead it on a floured worktop for 5 minutes until you have a smooth dough, wrap it in cling film and allow to rest for 20 minutes in the fridge.

While the dough is resting, make the filling. Mix the pork mince in a bowl with the spring onion, garlic, a splash of sesame oil and a splash of soy sauce.

To make it easier to work with, cut the dough in half (you'll probably have twice as much dough as you need, so freeze the rest, or make more gyoza! Double the filling quantities if you use all the dough).

Lightly dust half of the dough with flour and roll it out as thinly as possible with a rolling pin (or a pasta rolling machine).

Using the rim of a wine glass, cut out as many circles of pasta as you can and lay them on the worktop ready for filling. Dip a fingertip in water and run it around half the edge of a pasta circle. Spoon a small amount of the pork filling (about the size of an almond) into the centre and fold the pasta circle in half. Make sure there is no air trapped inside, then gently press the edges together to form a seal. Repeat with the rest of the pasta circles and filling.

Heat a frying pan until hot, add a splash of sesame oil, then fry your gyoza. After 1 minute, add a splash of water and place a lid (or upturned plate) on top.

Leave the gyoza to steam for about 3 minutes then, once the water has evaporated, continue to fry in the pan with no lid for a few more minutes until the pork is cooked through.

Serve with a soy sauce dip.

MEATBALL MARINARA

Channel your inner Italian mobster by tucking a napkin into your shirt and sitting down to this hearty plate of meatballs. It takes about 20 minutes to knock this up from scratch, making it an ideal mid-week meal. If you like these meatballs, try them in a sandwich (see page 142).

To make 1 portion

75g minced beef

1 tsp dried oregano

½ red onion, ¼ finely diced and ¼ sliced

1 garlic clove, ½ crushed and ½ sliced

125g dried spaghetti

200g passata

Small handful of grated Cheddar cheese

Olive oil

Salt and pepper

To cook

In a bowl, mix together the minced beef, half the oregano, the finely diced onion, and the crushed garlic, then season well. Squash everything together with your fingers and create 4 meatballs. Pan-fry the meatballs in a splash of olive oil over a medium heat and keep turning them until they take on a lovely deep brown colour.

Meanwhile, bring a saucepan of salted water to the boil and cook the spaghetti until al dente.

When the meatballs are cooked, add the sliced onion and sliced garlic to the pan (keep the meatballs in the pan). Fry until the garlic starts to colour, then add the passata, remaining oregano and some salt and pepper. Simmer for a few minutes to reduce the sauce slightly, then scatter over the cheese and melt under the grill.

Serve the meatballs with the spaghetti and don't forget to tuck your napkin into your shirt!

NEW YORK MEATBALL SANDWICH

This recipe was a huge hit on Instagram. It takes just 10 minutes to make and is a whole meal in a sandwich. When I was creating the recipe, I used a clever little technique for keeping the bread dry and away from the sauce. Firstly, I pan-toasted the bread to make it crunchier and less absorbent. Then, I took it one step further and melted cheese on one side of each slice, forming a neat little sauce-proof barrier and perfectly finishing off my decadent New York meatball sandwich. If you like the meatballs, have a look at my Meatball Marinara on the previous page.

To make 1 portion

75g minced beef

¼ red onion, finely diced

1 garlic clove, crushed

1 tsp dried oregano

2 slices of bread

Handful of grated Cheddar cheese

200g passata

Olive oil

Salt and pepper

To cook

In a bowl, mix the minced beef with the diced onion, half the crushed garlic and half the oregano, and season with salt and pepper. Form into 4 compact balls and pan-fry over a medium heat with a splash of olive oil until darkly coloured.

Meanwhile, toast the bread slices on both sides in a pan with a splash of olive oil, then sprinkle the grated cheese on one side of each slice and melt under the grill.

When the meatballs are cooked, add the passata to the pan, along with the remaining garlic, oregano and more salt and pepper (keep the meatballs in the pan), and simmer for 1–2 minutes to reduce the sauce slightly.

Make the sandwich with the cheese facing inwards and enjoy your very own taste of New York!

ULTIMATE £1 ROAST

This is the king of roasts! It looks like no expense has been spared, so how can this only cost £1? The reason is that you will have to work hard to turn these inexpensive ingredients into the ultimate roast. But it's Sunday and you've got all day, so why not have a little fun? If you like this, check out my posh Roast Chicken Ballotine and Potatoes on page 92.

To make 1 portion

3 tbsp dry stuffing mix

approx. 20ml water

1 chicken leg, bone in and skin on

1 large potato, peeled and cut into large chunks

A few Savoy cabbage leaves, cut into thin strips

1 tsp gravy granules

Olive oil

Salt and pepper

To cook

First, combine the stuffing mix with the water. Squash everything together using your fingers, then roll the stuffing into a cylindrical shape.

Next, debone the chicken leg, keeping the skin on, and season the inside well.

Lay the chicken leg skin-side down on a sheet of tin foil and place the stuffing in the middle. Wrap it tightly into a neat cylinder and twist each end of the foil to make it extra tight. Poach in boiling water for 25 minutes, then cool under cold running water and refrigerate for a minimum of 30 minutes (you can do this the night before).

When you are ready to cook your ultimate £1 roast, preheat the oven to 190°C/gas mark 5.

Rinse the potato chunks under cold running water, place in a pan of cold salted water and bring to the boil. Cook for roughly 10 minutes until they soften slightly (so you can pierce them with a fork but they do not break). Drain, then return them to the saucepan and drench them in a few very generous glugs of olive oil. Tip into a baking tray and roast for about 35 minutes, turning a couple of times, until golden and crispy.

While the potato cooks, peel the foil off the chicken and pan-fry it gently in a splash of olive oil over a low–medium heat for about 20 minutes. Keep turning the chicken with tongs to evenly brown the skin (make sure the chicken is hot throughout).

Just before serving, season and pan-fry the cabbage over a high heat for a couple of minutes in a splash of olive oil.

Mix the gravy granules with boiling water (according to the packet instructions) and enjoy your ultimate £1 roast.

ULTIMATE £1 HANGOVER CURE

One of the great unanswered questions of modern times is: how do you double the amount of cheese in a grilled cheese sandwich without it just spilling out of the sides? It took a book by Miguel Barclay to finally answer this question. The answer was simple. Bind it together with macaroni and be as reckless as you dare.

To make 1 portion

2 slices of bread

Butter, for spreading

Small handful of macaroni

Handful of grated mature Cheddar cheese

Splash of Worcestershire sauce

Tabasco sauce

Sprinkle of celery salt

Glass of tomato juice

Salt and pepper

To cook

Lightly butter both sides of the bread slices and gently pan-fry them until golden brown on both sides.

Meanwhile, bring a pan of salted water to the boil and cook the macaroni until al dente, then drain and return it to the empty saucepan. Add the grated cheese and gently stir, over a very low heat, until the cheese is fully melted.

Pile the macaroni cheese filling between the pieces of toasted bread and create the tallest cheese sandwich you possibly can.

For the Virgin Bloody Mary, add the Worcestershire sauce, some Tabasco sauce, celery salt and loads of pepper to the glass of tomato juice.

Forget all about last night as you tuck into your ultimate £1 hangover cure, then sit yourself in front of the telly with your duvet.

THAI CRAB CAKES & BISQUE

These Thai crab cakes are delicate, sweet and fluffy in texture. Served on a super-easy and simplified bisque, you'll be wondering how you managed to cook this dish in no time at all, and for under £1.

To make 1 portion

40g tinned crab

4 green beans, trimmed and finely chopped

1 egg, beaten

Small handful of breadcrumbs (grated stale bread)

1 garlic clove, crushed

Pinch of dried chilli flakes

200g chopped tomatoes (from a 400g tin)

½ fish stock cube

30ml single cream

Olive oil

Salt and pepper

To cook

In a bowl, mix the crab meat, chopped green beans, half the beaten egg (keep the rest of the beaten egg in the fridge for another recipe), breadcrumbs, garlic and chilli flakes. Season well.

Heat a frying pan over a medium heat with a splash of olive oil. Using a tablespoon, dollop little balls of crab mixture into the frying pan. Cook for about 15 minutes, turning the crab cakes occasionally, until lightly browned and cooked all the way through.

Meanwhile, in a separate pan, over a medium heat, add the chopped tomatoes and crumble in the fish stock cube. Season well and after a few minutes, when the sauce has reduced slightly, add the cream. Simmer for a further 1–2 minutes, then remove from the heat.

Serve the crab cakes on the bisque and enjoy!

MUSHROOM GNOCCHI

You have two options here: make your own gnocchi from scratch, or buy some from the shop. Either way, this dish still comes in at under £1, so tailor it according to how brave you are feeling, or how much time you have. I like to make my own gnocchi, and sometimes add a few random herbs to it, too.

To make 1 portion

Handful of shop-bought gnocchi
 (or 1 potato, 1 egg and 1 tbsp plain flour)

A few mushrooms, sliced

60ml single cream

Handful of grated parmesan, plus a few
 extra flakes

Olive oil

Salt and pepper

To cook

To make your own gnocchi, boil the peeled potato, drain and mash it, season, add the beaten egg, 1 tablespoon of flour and gently knead to form a dough. Roll into a sausage shape and cut into bite-sized pieces. Simple!

Place your gnocchi in a saucepan of salted boiling water and cook for a couple of minutes, then drain.

Meanwhile, pan-fry the mushrooms in a splash of olive oil until cooked, and season well. Add the gnocchi and the cream, then simmer for a minute to reduce the sauce slightly. Remove from the heat and stir in the grated parmesan.

Serve with a few extra flakes of parmesan to garnish.

GNOCCHI AL FORNO

Ever wondered what else you can do with gnocchi? Well, gnocchi is fantastic baked in the oven! If you don't have time to make it from scratch (see Mushroom Gnocchi recipe on page 150), you can buy it ready-made in most supermarkets and still make this dish for under £1. Just make this quick sauce, add some blue cheese, throw in some veg and you have a very posh sounding 'gnocchi al forno'.

To make 1 portion

½ onion, sliced

1 tsp plain flour

100ml milk

50g stilton cheese, crumbled

Handful of gnocchi (see page 150 if you want to make it yourself)

A few broccoli florets

Olive oil

To cook

Preheat your oven to 190°C/gas mark 5.

Gently fry the onion with a splash of olive oil in an ovenproof pan or casserole dish then, once it softens, stir in the flour and continue to cook for 1 minute. Next, add the milk very slowly, while continuing to stir, to create a thick sauce. Mix in the stilton cheese, then the gnocchi and broccoli florets.

Transfer to the oven and bake for about 20 minutes until the top is golden brown.

FAUX CONFIT CHICKEN

This is a traditional French dish typically made with confit duck legs, but duck is mega expensive, so this is my One Pound Meals version, which hits all the same flavour notes but at a fraction of the price. To try and replicate the confit effect, I score the meat to the bone, allowing it to separate during cooking, and then baste it multiple times in olive oil and give it a generous sprinkling of salt to create that amazing crispy texture. The lentils are prepared in a traditional French way, with bacon and veg, to complete the dish.

To make 1 portion

1 chicken leg, bone in and skin on

¼ onion, sliced

2 rashers of smoked streaky bacon, sliced

½ carrot, diced

1 garlic clove, sliced

½ tsp dried oregano

½ tsp plain flour

Handful of puy lentils

½ chicken stock cube

200ml water

Olive oil

Salt and pepper

To cook

Preheat your oven to 190°C/gas mark 5.

Take your chicken leg and, about 2cm from the end of the drumstick, cut a circle through the flesh all the way to the bone. Season well with salt and pepper and drizzle with olive oil.

Roast in the oven on a baking tray for about 40 minutes, basting it occasionally and sprinkling with more salt, until golden brown, crispy on the outside and cooked through.

Meanwhile, for the lentils, start by frying the sliced onion in a pan over a medium heat with a splash of olive oil until soft. Add the bacon and, when it starts to go crispy, add the carrot, garlic and oregano and season with salt and pepper. When the garlic starts to colour, stir in the flour, and when it has disappeared, add the lentils, crumble in the

chicken stock cube and add the water. Simmer for 15 minutes, or until the lentils are tender, adding more water if necessary.

When the chicken is cooked, serve it on a bed of the oozy French lentils and enjoy.

KEEMA BOMBAY POTATOES

When you're stuck for inventive ideas for minced beef, look no further than a satisfying keema dish. Here, I have merged it with a classic curried Bombay potato recipe to create 'keema Bombay potatoes'. This has everything you need – a lovely balance of meat, potatoes and veg – with plenty of flavour, too.

To make 1 portion

A few small potatoes, halved

100g minced beef

1 tbsp curry powder

½ onion, sliced

Handful of frozen peas

Olive oil

Salt and pepper

To cook

Cook the potatoes in a pan of salted boiling water until soft.

Meanwhile, season and fry the minced beef in a pan with a splash of olive oil over a medium heat. When the meat starts to brown, add the curry powder, onion and a splash more olive oil. Continue to fry for a few minutes, then add the drained cooked potatoes. Season once more, add the frozen peas, and continue to fry over a medium heat until everything is cooked.

Grab a fork and enjoy straight from the pan.

CHRISTMAS DINNER

This Christmas dinner proves just how much can be achieved with a £1 budget. With some clever cheats, you can transform a chicken leg into this stunning, picture-perfect Christmas meal for 1. Once you've mastered my technique, you'll love my Roast Chicken Ballotine (page 92) and Ultimate £1 Roast (page 144).

To make 1 portion

1 chicken leg, de-boned and skin on

½ red onion, finely diced

1 tsp cranberry sauce

Small handful of breadcrumbs (grated stale bread)

1 large potato, peeled and roughly chopped

3 tbsp dry stuffing mix

approx. 20ml water

1 rasher of smoked streaky bacon, cut widthways into 3 short strips

3 brussels sprouts, separated into leaves

1 tsp gravy granules

Olive oil

Salt and pepper

To cook

Lay the chicken skin-side down on a sheet of tin foil and stuff it with a mixture of the onion, cranberry sauce and breadcrumbs. Wrap it tightly into a neat cylinder and twist each end of the foil to create a Christmas cracker shape, then wrap 4 pieces of butcher's string around the chicken.

Poach in boiling water for 25 minutes, then cool under cold running water and chill for at least 30 minutes (you can do this the night before).

Preheat your oven to 190°C/gas mark 5.

Rinse the chopped potato under cold running water, place in a pan of cold salted water, bring to the boil and cook until soft. Drain, tip back into the empty saucepan and – while still steaming hot – drench in a few generous glugs of olive oil. Tip into a baking tray and roast for about 40 minutes, turning occasionally, until golden and crispy.

Mix the stuffing mix with the water to create a stuffing with the consistency of mashed potato. Roll it into 3 sausage shapes, wrap them in the bacon (secure them with toothpicks, if necessary) and cook in the oven on a separate baking tray for about 20 minutes.

Peel the foil off the chicken (don't remove the string) and pan-fry in a splash of oil for about 25 minutes, turning it with tongs to evenly brown the skin (make sure the chicken is hot throughout).

Just before serving, pan-fry the sprout leaves, seasoned generously, in a splash of oil.

Mix the gravy granules with boiling water (according to the packet instructions) and serve your ultimate £1 Christmas dinner.

CHRISTMAS BUTTERNUT SQUASH

If you are having trouble finding an inventive way to cook your vegetarian Christmas dinner this year, I bet you've never seen this before. For such a special day, making that extra effort with this fun and tasty dish is definitely worthwhile. Hooray, no more nut roast! Let's bring some Christmas cheer to your plate.

To make 1 portion

2cm-thick circular slice of butternut squash, peeled

1 large potato, peeled and roughly diced

Small handful of crumbled feta cheese

5 x 5cm sheet of puff pastry

3 brussels sprouts, separated into leaves

1 tsp vegetable gravy granules

Olive oil

Salt and pepper

To cook

Preheat your oven to 190°C/gas mark 5.

Season the squash, drizzle both sides with olive oil, then roast in the oven on a baking tray for 15 minutes.

Meanwhile, rinse the diced potato under cold running water, then place in a pan of cold salted water, bring to the boil and cook until soft. Drain, tip back into the empty saucepan and – while still steaming hot – toss with a few generous glugs of olive oil. Tip into a baking tray and roast for about 40 minutes, turning occasionally, until golden and crispy.

When the squash is roasted, let it cool, then top with the crumbled feta. Cut out Christmassy shapes from the puff pastry and place on top of the feta and squash.

About 15 minutes before the potatoes are ready, bake the squash and pastry shapes until the pastry starts to turn golden brown.

While the squash and potato are cooking, pan-fry the sprout leaves, seasoned generously, in a splash of oil.

Mix the gravy granules with boiling water (according to the packet instructions), then arrange everything beautifully on the plate to create your ultimate vegetarian Christmas dinner.

LAHMACUN

This recipe is a cross between a Turkish lahmacun and a Turkish pide. These are described in most guidebooks as simply 'Turkey's answer to pizza', but there is so much more to this dish than initially meets the eye. So, give it a go and judge for yourself.

To make 1 portion

40g plain flour, plus extra for dusting (if needed)

25ml cold water

1 tbsp passata

20g minced lamb

A few pieces of finely diced red onion

½ tsp ground cumin

½ tsp paprika

Pinch of dried parsley

Olive oil

Salt and pepper

To cook

Preheat your oven to 190°C/gas mark 5.

Mix the flour and water in a bowl with a pinch of salt. Once a dough has formed, knead for a minute on the worktop, dusting the dough with flour if it becomes too sticky. Roll the dough out into a 20cm circle, place on a baking tray, then roll the edges inwards slightly to form a rough oval shape.

Spread the passata onto the dough, then sprinkle with small chunks of minced lamb. Next, add some finely diced red onion, then sprinkle over the cumin and paprika. Drizzle over some olive oil and cook in the oven for 10–15 minutes until the edges are crispy and the lamb is cooked.

Season with salt and pepper and sprinkle with the dried parsley before serving.

PORK CHOP & COLCANNON

This is a One Pound Meal for men with big bushy beards and muscles! A real meat-and-two-veg classic. A chunky pan-fried pork chop with a cabbage and potato colcannon – this is simple and hearty grub at its very best.

To make 1 portion

1 large potato, peeled and quartered

1 pork chop

Handful of shredded Savoy cabbage

1 tsp butter

½ tsp plain flour

Olive oil

Salt and pepper

To cook

Cook the potato in salted boiling water until soft enough to pierce with a fork.

Meanwhile, season the pork chop then pan-fry it over a medium heat in a splash of oil for 7 minutes on each side, or until cooked all the way through.

While the pork chop is cooking, pan-fry the cabbage in a separate pan in a splash of olive oil over a medium heat. Season generously, then add a splash of water to help steam the cabbage. Continue to cook for 4 minutes until the cabbage is tender and the water has evaporated.

When the potatoes are cooked, drain, season and mash with the butter. Fold the cabbage through the mashed potato to create your colcannon.

When the pork chop is fully cooked, transfer it to a plate. Add the flour to the pan over a low heat, stirring it into the pan juices, then add a splash of water to create the gravy. Keep stirring and add a little more water if necessary.

Serve the pork chop with the colcannon on the side and smother it with the gravy.

SPANISH OMELETTE

Delicious hot or cold, this is a filling dish that would also make a great packed lunch: you never see people bringing a Spanish omelette to work, but it's perfect for eating on the go. Imagine tucking into one of these for tomorrow's lunch! So, next time you are wondering what to do with the last potato in the bag, don't have a baked potato, try a Spanish omelette. I've even simplified the recipe using a few of my One Pound Meals shortcuts, so there's really no excuse.

To make 1 portion

1 large potato, diced

20ml water

½ onion, diced

4 eggs

Olive oil

Salt and pepper

To cook

Throw the diced potato in a frying pan, add the water, cover with a lid (or large plate) and steam the potato for about 10 minutes over a medium heat.

Keep an eye on the pan and, once the water has evaporated, remove the lid and throw in the diced onion, a good glug of olive oil and season very generously. Fry over a medium heat until the potato and onion start to colour. At this point, turn the heat down to the lowest setting and crack the eggs into the pan. Mix everything together and cook the omelette very slowly for 10–15 minutes.

Once about 80 per cent of the omelette is cooked, just finish off the top under the grill.

LEEK & BACON GRATIN

Here, I have taken the flavours and techniques from one of my favourite French side dishes and added my own One Pound Meals twist. Instead of the usual posh thinly sliced boiled potatoes, I've used chunky halved new potatoes and left the skin on. Instead of sliced white onions hiding in the background, I've used chunky chopped leeks and brought them into the foreground of the dish, and along with the addition of crispy smoked bacon, have elevated it to main-course status!

To make 1 portion

Handful of new potatoes, halved

½ leek, roughly chopped

4 rashers of smoked streaky bacon, roughly chopped

100ml single cream

1 garlic clove, crushed

Handful of grated mature Cheddar cheese

Olive oil

Salt and pepper

To cook

Preheat your oven to 190°C/gas mark 5.

Boil the new potatoes in a pan of salted water until cooked all the way through.

Meanwhile, gently pan-fry the leek and bacon in a splash of olive oil over a medium heat. When the bacon starts to crisp up, remove from the heat.

When the potatoes are cooked, drain and tip them into an ovenproof dish, adding the cooked leeks and bacon, plus the cream, garlic and grated cheese. Stir and season, then cook in the oven for about 25 minutes until the top is a lovely golden brown. Remove from the oven and dig in!

SPICED BUTTERNUT SQUASH SOUP

Butternut squash is amazing value for money. When you consider its size next to a comparatively priced avocado or aubergine, it's huge! It's also delicious, versatile and filling, so that makes it a very useful main ingredient when eating on a budget (have a look at my Butternut Squash Risotto on page 32 or Tagliatelle on page 60). In this recipe, I oven-roast it in paprika to create a sweet and spicy soup that will definitely excite your taste buds. Serve with some lovely crusty bread.

To make 1 portion

½ butternut squash, peeled and diced

2 tsp paprika

100ml water

½ vegetable stock cube

Slice of crusty bread

Olive oil

Salt and pepper

To cook

Preheat your oven to 190°C/gas mark 5.

Toss the squash in an ovenproof dish with a generous glug of olive oil and half the paprika, and season with salt and pepper. Add a few of the butternut squash seeds too – when they roast in the oven they become deliciously crunchy and are great to scatter over the top of the soup for an interesting contrast in texture.

Roast for 40 minutes until soft and gooey. Remove from the oven and keep the roasted seeds, some of the paprika-infused oil and a few pieces of squash aside for garnishing. Then, blend the rest of the baked squash with the water, crumbled stock cube and the rest of the paprika to create a thick, satisfying soup.

Season to taste, pour into a bowl, and add the chunks of squash along with the seeds and paprika-infused oil to finish the dish.

PRAWN & FETA BRÛLÉE

Topping oven-baked dishes with garlicky breadcrumbs is always delicious, but when you then add melted cubes of feta cheese, you're onto a winner – it's a great way of elevating everyday ingredients into a mouthwatering dish. In this recipe, prawns are contrasted with soft tangy cheese and crunchy breadcrumbs to create an almost gratin-style brûlée that keeps you digging in for more.

To make 1 portion

¼ red onion, diced

2 garlic cloves, 1 chopped and 1 crushed

200g chopped tomatoes (from a 400g tin)

50g cooked and peeled prawns

50g feta cheese, cubed

Handful of breadcrumbs (grated stale bread)

Olive oil

Salt and pepper

To cook

Preheat your oven to 190°C/gas mark 5.

Gently pan-fry the diced onion in a splash of oil over a medium heat for a few minutes, until softened. Add the chopped garlic and continue to fry until the garlic starts to brown. Add the chopped tomatoes, season and simmer for a couple of minutes then remove from the heat, transfer to an ovenproof dish and add the prawns and feta.

Add the crushed garlic clove to the breadcrumbs with a splash of olive oil and season with salt and pepper. Mix with your fingers, then sprinkle liberally over the dish.

Cook in the oven for 30 minutes, or until the breadcrumbs are golden brown, remove from the oven and serve in the dish. Grab a fork and dig in!

SPANAKOPITA PIE

Spanakopita is a classic Greek dish that sandwiches a thick layer of garlic-infused spinach and crumbly feta between many layers of filo pastry, each individually brushed with melted butter during assembly. But I thought this was way too much effort, so gave this dish a One Pound Meals makeover and encased it in a puff pastry pie!

To make 1 portion

¼ onion, diced

1 garlic clove, sliced

Handful of spinach

25g feta cheese, crumbled

1 egg, beaten

Sheet of puff pastry

Olive oil

Salt and pepper

To cook

Preheat your oven to 190°C/gas mark 5.

Gently pan-fry the onion in a splash of olive oil over a medium heat. As the onion starts to brown, add the garlic and continue to fry. Once the garlic starts to brown, add the spinach and as soon as it starts to wilt, stir through the feta cheese and egg. Remove from the heat and tip into a small ovenproof dish.

Cut a square of puff pastry the same size as the ovenproof dish and cover the spinach mixture, then cook it in the oven for 30 minutes, or until the pastry is a lovely golden brown colour.

Remove from the oven and tuck in.

LAMB KOFTE WITH FLATBREAD

These lamb koftas are delicious! They are so simple to make, but packed with flavour. You can add whatever salad you have left in the fridge, then just wrap them up and enjoy!

To make 1 portion

100g minced lamb

½ red onion, ¼ diced and ¼ sliced

1 tsp ground cumin

40g plain flour

25ml cold water

10g feta cheese, crumbled

Olive oil

Salt and pepper

To cook

In a bowl, mix the minced lamb with the diced onion and cumin and some salt and pepper. Squash together with your fingers and form into kebabs around 2 skewers (soak the skewers in water beforehand if using wooden ones).

Preheat a griddle pan over a high heat. Lightly brush each kebab with oil, then cook on the griddle pan for about 5 minutes, turning the kebabs every so often ensuring they are cooked through and all sides have charred grill marks.

While the kebabs are cooking, make the flatbread. Mix the flour, water and a pinch of salt in a bowl to form a dough. Knead for a minute on the worktop then roll it out into a rough 20cm circle. Cook in a dry frying pan over a high heat for 2 minutes on each side until nicely toasted.

Place the kebabs in the flatbread and serve with the sliced onion and crumbled feta.

MOROCCAN LETTUCE TACOS

Although this is a totally made-up dish, the different inspirations work so well together. I love the dark depth of flavour from the Moroccan seasoned lamb that contrasts so perfectly with the tangy feta cheese and sweet crispy lettuce. Maybe Moroccan Lettuce Tacos could be a real dish?

To make 1 portion

¼ red onion, diced

75g minced lamb

1 tsp ground cumin

1 tsp paprika

A few Baby Gem lettuce leaves

10g feta cheese, crumbled

Olive oil

Salt and pepper

To cook

Pan-fry the diced red onion gently in a splash of olive oil over a medium heat. When it starts to soften, add the lamb, cumin and paprika. Season and continue to fry for about 10 minutes until everything is nicely dark and caramelised.

Spoon the lamb mixture into lettuce leaves to create a taco effect, then scatter over the crumbled feta cheese to finish.

ASPARAGUS MESS

This dish is so cool, and it tastes amazing too. This is one of my favourite styles of cooking – sort of rustic but clean and fresh at the same time. It's so quick to whip up and so tasty that you'll be looking forward to asparagus season all year: as soon as the season hits, prices plummet and you can eat this dish every day!

To make 1 portion

2 dried lasagne sheets

Handful of asparagus spears, cut in half

1 tbsp crème fraîche

Grated zest and juice of ½ lemon

Grating of parmesan

Olive oil

Salt and pepper

To cook

Cook the lasagne sheets and asparagus spears in a saucepan of salted boiling water until the lasagne sheets are floppy and the asparagus is tender.

The asparagus will be done first, so remove the spears and start to pan-fry them in a splash of olive oil over a medium heat. After 1 minute, season the asparagus with salt and pepper, add the crème fraîche, a squeeze of lemon juice, a little of the lemon zest and a sprinkling of grated parmesan. After 1 minute, remove from the heat and make sure everything is mixed together nicely.

Roughly arrange a lasagne sheet on a plate so it is crumpled and uneven, spoon half the asparagus mixture on top, then arrange the other lasagne sheet in the same fashion. Top with the remaining asparagus, drizzle a little olive oil over the top, and scatter over the remaining lemon zest and some more grated parmesan for the final flourish.

THAI RED CHICKEN CURRY

Every household needs a favourite Thai curry recipe, and my One Pound Meals version of this classic dish is super-easy and delicious. Give it a try and see just how quick and simple this recipe actually is. Everything is cooked in one pan and all the flavours are mixed together during the cooking process, so there's no need to make elaborate pastes – just grab a tin of coconut milk and the rest of the dish is made up of regular everyday ingredients.

To make 1 portion

1 chicken thigh, de-boned and diced

4 charlotte potatoes, halved

2 spring onions, sliced

2 tsp paprika

200ml coconut milk (from a 400g tin)

½ chicken stock cube

200ml water

Olive oil

Salt and pepper

To cook

Start by frying the diced chicken thigh in a saucepan with a splash of oil over a medium heat, season well, and once the chicken starts to brown, add the potatoes and most of the sliced spring onions. After a few minutes, add the paprika and coconut milk, crumble in the stock cube and add the water.

Simmer gently for 20 minutes until the sauce is thickened and the potatoes are soft.

Serve garnished with the remaining spring onion.

How easy was that?

SPAGHETTI CARBONARA

A classic Italian carbonara has a luxurious silky sauce but is actually made without cream. By using a clever technique involving the leftover pasta water, this dish is a great example of how to get the most out of your ingredients while keeping your costs down. And, don't forget to save the egg whites – they'll come in useful for another dish (maybe egg white omelette for breakfast? That's a free meal!).

To make 1 portion

¼ onion, diced

3 rashers of smoked streaky bacon, diced

100g mushrooms, sliced

125g dried spaghetti

2 egg yolks

Handful of grated parmesan (approx. 12g), plus extra to serve (optional)

Olive oil

Salt and pepper

To cook

Bring a large pan of salted water to the boil.

Pan-fry the onion over a medium heat in a splash of olive oil. After a few minutes, add the bacon and continue to fry for a few more minutes before adding the mushrooms.

Now, cook the spaghetti in the salted boiling water until al dente.

Once the bacon is starting to crisp up and the mushrooms are cooked, remove the frying pan from the heat and set to one side.

While the spaghetti is cooking, mix the egg yolks with the parmesan in a bowl and add lots of cracked black pepper.

Once the spaghetti is cooked, using tongs, transfer it to the bowl and start stirring it into the egg yolks and parmesan mixture. The heat from the pasta will start to cook the egg and by adding just a few tablespoons of the starchy pasta water you will see it transform into a delicious silky smooth sauce.

Mix in the onion, bacon and mushroom mixture, and serve immediately on a warm plate.

Garnish with a grating of parmesan, if you like, and enjoy!

ARANCINI WITH GARLIC & CHILLI TOMATO SAUCE

Arancini is traditionally a humble way to use up leftover risotto, but in recent years they have become so popular that restaurants have sprung up specialising exclusively in this Italian delicacy! Here, I have made a simple parmesan risotto from scratch, but you could use leftover risotto (try my Mushroom Risotto on page 130).

To make 1 portion (3 arancini)

¼ onion, diced

Handful of Arborio risotto rice (approx. 125g)

500ml boiling water

1 stock cube

Handful of grated parmesan

1 garlic clove, sliced

Pinch of dried chilli flakes

100g passata

1 tbsp plain flour

1 egg, beaten

Handful of breadcrumbs (grated stale bread)

3 small chunks of mozzarella

Vegetable oil

Olive oil

Salt and pepper

To cook

Start by sticking the kettle on.

Pan-fry the onion in a splash of olive oil for 5 minutes. Before it browns, stir in the rice and season.

Add 100ml of the hot water from the kettle and crumble in the stock cube. Stir over a medium heat as the stock cube dissolves.

After a few minutes, the rice will have absorbed most of the water. Keep adding hot water, 100ml at a time, as you continue to stir. After about 20 minutes, the rice should be tender but still al dente. Remove from the heat and stir in the parmesan.

While the rice cools, create your sauce. Gently pan-fry the garlic and chilli flakes in a splash of olive oil. Just before the garlic browns, add the passata and simmer while you make the arancini.

Preheat the deep-fat fryer, or carefully heat some vegetable oil (about 5cm deep) in a saucepan.

Place seasoned flour in one bowl, the egg in another bowl, and seasoned breadcrumbs in a third bowl.

Flatten a tablespoon of the cold risotto in the palm of your hand, then wrap it around a chunk of mozzarella. Roll it in the flour, then the egg, and finally the breadcrumbs. Repeat with the remaining risotto and mozzarella chunks.

Fry the arancini, no more than two at a time, for about 10 minutes, until golden brown, and serve with your garlic and chilli tomato sauce. Buon appetito!

CHICKEN CAESAR SALAD

This simple Caesar salad is phenomenal! It has a lovely tangy dressing that brings everything together nicely to create my favourite version of this classic dish. It is also a useful dish for using up old bread, so next time you're about to throw some out, save it for this Caesar salad and make yourself some deliciously crunchy croutons.

To make 1 portion

1 chicken thigh, de-boned

1 tbsp mayo

½ garlic clove, crushed

Squeeze of lemon juice

Big pinch of grated parmesan cheese, plus shavings to garnish (use a potato peeler)

A few chunks of stale bread

A few Baby Gem lettuce leaves

Olive oil

Salt and pepper

To cook

Season and gently pan-fry the chicken thigh skin-side down in a splash of olive oil over a medium heat for 7 minutes, then a further 7 minutes on the other side, until golden brown and cooked through.

Meanwhile, for the sauce, mix together the mayo, crushed garlic, lemon juice, grated parmesan, a splash of olive oil and plenty of cracked black pepper in a bowl.

For the croutons, either chop or tear the chunks of bread into a pan, add a generous glug of olive oil and season with salt and loads of pepper. Pan-fry them over a high heat until they are evenly coloured on all sides and crisp.

In a bowl, arrange some lettuce leaves, add the croutons, then scatter parmesan shavings over the top. Add the pan-fried chicken then smother the salad in that gorgeous Caesar dressing.

TEMPURA PRAWNS & VEGETABLES

This is one of my guilty pleasures. By using little broccoli florets and other finely trimmed veg, the dish has a lovely delicate nature. The tempura batter is so simple and costs only a few pence to make, too – it is literally just self-raising flour, water and salt – so push the boat out and buy the biggest prawns you can find. Use any veg you have in the fridge but I really recommend trying the spring onions – it's not something you ever see, but they are my absolute favourite.

To make 1 portion

150g self-raising flour

200ml cold water

8 cooked and peeled prawns

4 small broccoli florets

4 baby carrots

2 spring onions, trimmed and each cut lengthways into 4 pieces

4 slices of courgette

Soy sauce

Vegetable oil

Salt

To cook

Turn on the deep-fat fryer to pre-heat, or heat some vegetable oil (about 3cm deep) in a saucepan.

Whisk the self-raising flour with the water and a pinch of salt in a bowl. Drop a tiny bit of batter into the oil to test it is hot enough – it should sizzle and turn golden brown.

Dip the prawns and veg into the batter, then fry them in batches for 1–2 minutes until light golden brown and crisp. Drain on kitchen paper and serve immediately, with a scattering of salt and a small bowl of soy sauce for dipping.

PARSNIP SOUP WITH OVEN-ROASTED ONION

I love oven-roasted onions, simply baked with a splash of olive oil and a generous pinch of salt and pepper. Why don't I ever see them anywhere? They are so easy to make and so delicious, and in this particular dish, they really help transform this parsnip soup from a starter into an amazing main course.

To make 1 portion

1 red onion, quartered

½ white onion, diced

2 parsnips, diced

½ vegetable stock cube

200ml milk

Olive oil

Salt and pepper

To cook

Preheat your oven to 190°C/gas mark 5.

Roast the quartered red onion in a baking tray with a splash of olive oil and a generous sprinkling of salt and pepper until cooked and slightly charred.

Meanwhile, in a saucepan, fry the diced white onion in a splash of olive oil over a medium heat. Season well, and as soon as the onion starts to soften, but before it has time to colour, add the parsnips, crumble in the stock cube and add the milk. Simmer for 20 minutes, then liquidise in a blender. If you find the soup too thick (its thickness will depend on how much liquid evaporated during the simmering stage), just add more milk or water.

Give it a taste and one last season with salt and pepper, pour into a bowl and arrange the roasted red onions on top. Add a little swirl of olive oil and a tiny amount of cracked black pepper to serve.

CORNISH PASTY

Learning to make shortcrust pastry unlocks the door to a whole new array of dishes. And one of my favourites has to be a homemade Cornish pasty. It's such a simple dish, with honest flavours, seasoned with just salt and pepper, and the filling entirely cooked inside the pastry. It also makes for an exciting alternative to your usual packed lunch (try out my Quiche Lorraine on page 106, too). Great with a big dollop of mustard.

To make 1 portion

100g plain flour

50g chilled butter

20ml cold water

25g minced beef

¼ onion, diced

¼ potato, diced

¼ carrot, diced

Salt and pepper

To cook

Preheat your oven to 190°C/gas mark 5.

In a bowl, combine the flour and butter by gently crumbling them together between your fingertips until the mixture resembles damp sand. Add the water and knead very gently to form a soft dough.

Transfer the dough to a worktop and roll it out to a disc roughly 20cm in diameter and about the thickness of a £1 coin.

Combine the minced beef in a bowl with the onion, potato and carrot and season well. Place the filling on the pastry, slightly off centre, then fold the dough in half – over the filling – to create a semi-circle.

Press the edges together to form a seal and crimp the pasty by folding the edge over itself repeatedly.

Pierce a hole at the top to allow the steam to escape and cook in the oven on a non-stick baking tray for about 45 minutes, until the pastry is nicely golden brown and the filling is cooked.

PORK CHOP IN A MUSTARD & LEEK SAUCE

Although the pork chop is the star ingredient here, what defines this dish is the tangy mustard and leek sauce. By using flour to thicken the sauce instead of cream, you can create this classic sauce at a fraction of the cost. Although the science behind the technique of thickening is quite complex, the method is so super-simple that you'll be tempted to whip this sauce up at every occasion. Give it a go with your next Sunday roast.

To make 1 portion

½ leek, rinsed and roughly chopped

1 pork chop

1 tsp wholegrain mustard

1 tsp plain flour

100ml milk

Olive oil

Salt and pepper

To cook

Heat a splash of olive oil in a saucepan over a medium heat, add the chopped leek, season and cook until softened.

While the leek is cooking, season the pork chop on both sides and fry it in a splash of oil over a medium heat for 7 minutes on each side until cooked all the way through.

Once the leeks are lovely and soft, add the wholegrain mustard and flour, then stir for a minute. Next, add the milk very slowly, while continuing to stir: a beautifully creamy sauce will appear before your very eyes!

Remove the saucepan and frying pan from the heat. Allow the pork chop to rest for a few minutes then serve it with the creamy mustard and leek sauce.

INDEX

First published in 2017
HEADLINE PUBLISHING GROUP

1

Cataloguing in Publication Data is available from the British Library

Hardback ISBN 9781472245618
eISBN 9781472245625

Commissioning Editor: Muna Reyal
Art Direction and Design: Superfantastic
Photography: Dan Jones
Project Editor: Kate Miles
Copy Editor: Laura Nickoll
Proofreader: Ilona Jasiewicz
Indexer: Caroline Wilding

HEADLINE PUBLISHING GROUP
An Hachette UK Company
Carmelite House
50 Victoria Embankment
London EC4Y 0DZ

www.headline.co.uk
www.hachette.co.uk

Thank you Dan, Sophie, Tamara, Muna & Mark